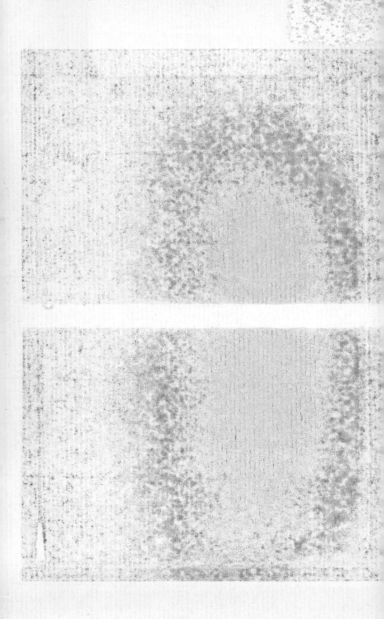

ENGLISH RECUSANT LITERATURE
1558–1640

Selected and Edited by
D. M. ROGERS

Volume 319

ROBERT, PRIOR OF SHREWSBURY
The Admirable Life of Saint Wenefride
1635

ROBERT, PRIOR OF SHREWSBURY

The Admirable Life of Saint Wenefride

1635

The Scolar Press

1976

ISBN 0 85967 333 2

Published and printed in Great Britain by
The Scolar Press Limited, 59-61 East Parade,
Ilkley, Yorkshire and
39 Great Russell Street,
London WC1

NOTE

Reproduced (original size) from a copy in the Bodleian Library, by permission of the Curators.

References: Allison and Rogers 725; STC 21102.

S.T WINEFRIDS WELL.

THE
ADMIRABLE LIFE
OF
S. WENEFRIDE,
VIRGIN, MARTYR,
Abbesse, & Patronesse
of Wales.

Permissu Superiorum
Anno 1635.

Mart: Bas:f.

THE

ADMIRABLE LIFE

OF SAINT

VVENEFRIDE

Virgin, Martyr, Abbeſſe.

Written in Latin aboue 500. yeares
ago, by ROBERT, Monke and
Priour of *Shrewsbury*, of the Ven.
Order of S. BENEDICT.

Deuided into two Bookes.

And now tranſlated into Engliſh, out
of a very ancient and authenticall
Manuſcript, for the edification and
comfort of Catholikes.

By I. F. of the Society of IESVS.

*Her memory is worthily honoured amongſt
Men, whoſe Soule is paſſed to the ioyes
of Angells. S. Max. hom. in S. Euſeb.*

Permiſſu Superiorū M.DC.XXXV.

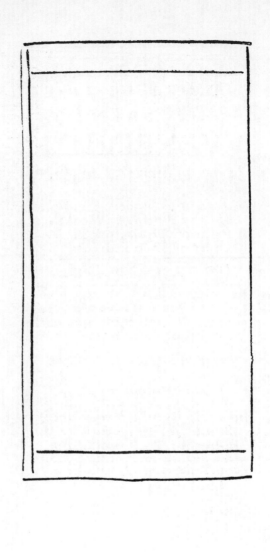

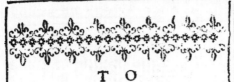

T O
THE NOBLE
GENTLEWOMAN
his Vertuous, & much
Honored friend,
M^rs.
DOROTHY BARLOW.

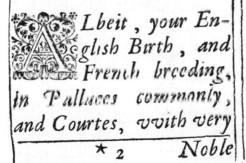

*A*Lbeit, your En-
glish Birth, and
French breeding,
in *Pallaces commonly*,
and *Courtes*, *vvith very*

* 2   *Noble*

Noble and Princely La-
dies, *haue made You a*
Stranger to Wales *for the*
greatest part of your life;
yet your Marriage *since,*
vvith a chiefe Gentleman
of that Country, and many
Children borne there (li-
uing partes of your selfe,
as that great Prince of Phi-
losophers *calleth them)*
may vvorthily make me
repute you S. Wenefrides
Countrey-vvoman.

Your singular Deuo-
tion

tion *besides*, to that re-
novvned Saint, and *great*
Patronesse *of* WALES,
vvhich lately caused you
(*as I haue heard*) to measure, *vvith no fevv* At-
tendants *of friends and*
seruants *about you*, *the*
vvhole length of that
Countrey, to visit *the de-*
uout & *memorable* Place
of *her* Martyrdome, ad-
ded *to that former* Res-
pect, *and a constant desire*
vvithall *in my selfe*, to

$\star$ 3   honour

honour, in vvhat I may,
& serue you; haue povver-
fully preuayled, & moued
me to present this translated *Life* of that glorious
VIRGIN, ABBESSE
and MARTYR, espe-
cially vnto you.

VVho as a bright mor-
ning-star ceaseth not euen
novv, to shyne, in her
ovvne knovvne Graces,
and daily Honours *done*
by deuout people vnto her;
vvhen as other Stars, in

this

this late darkenes, ouer-
vvhelming our Countrey,
are quite vanished out of
liuing mẽs sights: I meane,
innumerable Men, and
VVomen of Wales, very
conspicuous in tymes past,
for their admired Sancti-
ty, and honoured in Chur-
ches dedicated particularly vnto them, are novv
vtterly forgotten, and neuer againe, as knovvne
Saints, to be honoured by
vs, vntil in glory vve shall

come

come to behould their Soules first (if vve make our selues vvorthy of that happines, by a neere practise and perfect imitation of their Vertues) and Bodies aftervvards, out of their novv contemned, and trampled ashes, resplendently raysed.

And this Day-star of ours S. Wenefride, still shining in the Glory of her Merits, after other Saintes memories are past, and

Monu-

Monuments defaced, may haue, perchance, a happy Relation (as the naturall Day-starr hath to the rising Sunne) to an ending of this Darke Night of Religions, different from that, anciently by her, and holily professed, (vvherin likevvise her ovvne, and other Saintes Shrines, haue byn lamentably defaced) by a vvished restoring of Catholique Religion, vvhich as an heauen-

ly Light *hath ſcarſly euer beene obſcured, in your ovvne, or your Husbands ancient Families.*

A rare Happines in theſe tymes, and to fevv Houſes of Noble note, ſo graciouſly affoarded by the Authour of all Graces, vvhereby, their earthly Worth, hath vvith heauenly Graces ben happily matched; and are ſo eminently novv graced, by Your ovvne particular

Ver-

Vertues, as S. Wen fride *vvill gladly accepe such a Patronesse of hert Life printed, vvho so holily imitateth the same, as it vvas acted by her.* VVherin her *Blessed Intercession hath already, and vvill I doubt not, perseuerantly assiste you, by obteyning of her Diuine Spouse, Temporall Blessings, and Eternall Graces, for you and yours; vvhich I daily vvish, and hartily pray for,*

for, *as your euer deuoted friend, and seruant,*

In Christ IESVS,

I. F

T H E

THE
TRANSLATOVRS
PREFACE
TO HIS READER.

AMongſt many people Apoſtolically conuerted to the Fayth of Chriſt, the *Britans* or ancient Inhabitants of England, are vndoubtedly to be numbred, as *Origen* 4. *in Ezechielem*, *Tertullian contra Iudæos*, *Dorotheus* in his *Synopſis*, *Theodoret*, and others haue expreſly affirmed, beſides many home proofes, and pregnant teſtimonies of that their ſo

timely

timely conuerfion. Which primi
tiue Fayth of theirs hauing byn,
by a continuall mixture of Ro-
mans, and other Infidells liuing
amongſt them, and perfecuting
them for the fame, exceedingly
decayed; was againe cultiuated
by *Fugatius*, and *Damianus* Apo-
ſtolicall Preachers, fent for that
purpofe by Pope *Elutherius* vnto
them, the very next age after the
Apoſtles.

Since which tyme albeit they
loſt to the Saxons, the greateſt, &
fruitefulleſt part of their Country, and were enforced to betake
themfelues to the mountanous
places of *Wales* (as now it is called) and *Cornewall*; yet haue they
ſtill vntill this laſt age, vnalte-
redly maintayned their primitiue
Fayth, and Religion, as in the firſt

two

two Chapters of the Proteſtants Apology for the Roman Church, written by that learned man *M. Brerely*, is moſt cleerly proued, & demonſtrated.

And to recompence perhaps, their Conſtancy therein, and ſufferings for it, they were bleſſed from tyme to tyme with great numbers of *Saintes*, flouriſhing amongſt them; ſo as many Pariſhes in *Wales* and *Cornewall*, retayne no other names at this day, then ſuch as anciently they receaued from holy Men and Women liuing in them. Amongſt all which no one was for ſanctity & miraculous teſtimonies thereof, more then *S. Wenefride* famouſly renowned; and her Monuments now after a generall vaſtation of Monaſteries, and Saintes memo-

ries

ries in our Countrey, remayne vndefaced, and no lesse glorious in *Wales* and *England*, then *S. Catherines* Tombe on *Mount Sinai*, amongst fierce *Mahometans* and *Paynims*, is straungely, yet con serued.

And as the Sepulcher of that renowned Saint, is by faithfull people in those Easterne parts of the world Religiously visited: so in like manner do multitudes of holy Pilgrims frequently now resort vnto the place of *S. Wenefrids* martyrdome, & wonder to see such a floud of Cristall pure Water gushing there at once, out of the Earth, and a most sumptuous Chappell standing yet ouer it. So that the three Fountaynes neere *Rome*, which issued miraculously out of the ground, where *S. Paul*

was

was martyred, are not by much ſo curiouſly with building couered.

Moreouer, the waters of this holy Well, ſeeme to haue in thē more then naturall vertues, by giuing a musky, and moſt delightfull ſweetnes to the greene moſſe growing on the wals of this ſtately incloſure, and colouring all the ſtones which lye in the bottome thereof, with ſpots, as it were, of pure bloud, in them ſtrangly appearing. Many miracles alſo haue ben done heeretofore to manifeſt the ſanctity of this place; which becauſe they haue not ben by depoſitions of perſons ſworne, and publique Inſtruments authentically approued, I forbeare heere further to mention, then as my Authour doth afterwards recount them;

⁎⁎   and

and will only fay, that this Venerable and Coftly monument, is the more to be admired, for that it ftandeth in fo hilly, poore, and barren a Countrey, which hath fcarfly any thing, but this fayre building remarkable in it, exactly therefore drawne out by *M. Speed* in his Table of *Flint-fhyre*, and in his Comment hiftorically declared; yet with this tale ridiculoufly added, that Catholiques vifiting the *Well*, do really belieue the rednes of the ftones to be the Martyrs very bloud, and the Moffe growing therein her hayre, like to one of *Ouids* Metamorphofing Fables.

The Life of this Noble Virgin and Martyr, was diligently and authentically gathered (as himfelfe in his Prologue profeffeth)

by

by *Robertus Salopienſis*, a learned
Monke and *Priour* of *Shrewsbury*,
of the holy order of S. Benedict,
liuing in King *Stephens* tyme, &
for his great ſincerity, by *Cardi-
nall Baronius, Surius, Capgraue, Pits,
Poſseuinus*, and others, worthily
commended. Whoſe booke cop-
pied truly out of an old authenticall Manuſcript, I haue heere in
ſenſe faithfully tranſlated, and
done no otherwiſe in altering the
Authors old phraſes, ſcarſely ex-
preſſible in good Engliſh, then as
if I had ſtripped ſome body out of
Welſh courſe frize, and put him
into a ſuite of Engliſh playne
Kareſay.

And if the matter of the Booke,
conteyning in it ſundry ſtrange
and miraculous paſſages, ſhall
ſeeme ridiculous to *Proteſtant*

** 2   chan-

chancing to read them, it is not much to be wondred at, sithence they will be their owne choosers, euen in the very beliefe of sacred Verities themselues, diuinely reuealed; and sleight, as fabulous Legends, the Liues of Saintes, written by *S. Athanasius*, *S. Ambrose*, *S. Hierome*, *S. Climachus*, *S. Gregory*, and other holy Fathers.

It sufficed my Author, and so it shall me, that deuout Catholiques for whose instruction and comfort he penned first his Historie, will piously and probably assent to that, which heere is credibly proposed vnto them, auoyding two extremes therein; the one is of belieuing things ouerlightly, & the other of belieuing nothing at all but as fancies, and selfe-opinions do guide them. The which,

in

in Sectaries following commonly
this latter extreme in their iudg
ment of Catholique writings, is
a kind of Infidelity, and Impiety
mixed togeather: for if God be
wonderfull in his Saintes (as the
Royall Prophet telleth vs, *Psal.*
67.) and Christ in his Ascension
towards heauen did so expresly
promise, that these signes should
follow such as did belieue in him,
In my name (said he) they shall cast
out Diuells, they shall speake with
new tongues &c. why should we
vpon probable testimonies refuse
to belieue, such wonders to haue
ben done by Saintes, as diuine te-
stifications of their true Fayth,
and great graces heere obtayned?

The sacred body of this Virginall Blessed Saint, was solemnly
translated to *Shrewsbury* in this

* • 3   Au-

Authors tyme in the yeare of our Lord 1138. and raigne of *K. Stephen*, and there, in his owne Abbey magnificently interred, that greater honour and veneration, in so populous, and Religious a Citty (as that was then) might be yielded vnto it; where it conti nued, for aboue 400. yeares, till Herelie preuayled vtterly to ouerthrow in our Country the publique profession of Catholique Religion, and deface the Venerable monuments thereof euery where almost then extant. In which cōmon ruine & calamity hapning, the shrine of this great Saint with numbers of others became sacrilegiously defaced, and her sacred Reliques lye since disperfed God knoweth where or how, vntill by his omnipotency, they shall come

to be vnited againe, & moſt gloriouſly rayſed, *For God* (ſayth the
ſame holy Prophet *Pſal. 33.*) *doth*
conſerue all the bones of his ſeruants:
and it hath increaſed I doubt not
their ioyes accidentall in heauen,
to haue had heere on earth for his
ſake, their Reliques by the Churches enemies, and haters of true
Religion contemptucuſly abuſed,
after due Reuerence yeilded by
deuout people vnto them, and
ſingular bleſſings receaued from
Almighty God by their powerfull
interceſſion.

Neither haue moderne Sectaries ſhewed in any one act more,
the little Communion, which
they haue in this world, or are
likely to haue in the other, with
the Saintes of Chriſts Church,
then in contemning, ſcattering,

and destroying their Reliques, of which in generall *S. Ambrose* writeth thus, *Serm. 93. de Sanctis Nazario & Celso.* *If thou aske me what I honour in their flesh and bones now dissolued and consumed? I honour in the Martyrs flesh, the scarres of those woundes, which for Christ he susteyned; I honour the memory of his vertue still liuing; I honour in his ashes the seedes of Eternity; I honour the body that taught me to loue Christ, and not to feare the cruellest death for him. Why should not faithfull soules honour that body, which Diuells tremble at?* &c. *quod Christum honorauit in gladio, quod cum Christo regnabit in cælo: that body, I say, which honored Christ in the sword, and which shall reigne with him in Heauen. These* (sayth *S. Basill* speaking of the 40. Martyrs Reliques *) are those*

who

who protect our Countrey, and like strong Towers guard vs from our enemies .

Wherefore I may vfe, of fuch as fcattered, and deftroyed the holy reliques of *S.Wenefride*, and many other Saintes in our Country, *S.Gregory Nazianzens* words in his firft Oration againft *Iulian* the Apoftata ; *Thou haft not reuerenced the Hoaftes flaine for Chrift, whofe bodies, yea very drops of their bloud, or other fmall fignes of their paffions, can worke the fame effects which their foules themfelues can doe;* to wit fuch fudaine cures of infirmities and difeafes, as *S.Auftin lib. 22.de Ciuitate Dei cap. 8.* affirmeth by *S. Stephens* Reliques, as they paffed through *Afrique* towards *Rome*, to haue byn done in his prefence: which Proteftants will

as little belieue, as they do the miraculous paſſages of *S. Wenefride*
recounted in this Hiſtorie, a-
mongſt whome there is no one
ſo ſtraunge, but the like may be
found in other Saintes liues, by
holy & ancient Fathers authen
tically written; and in ſome of
them far more ſtraunge: which
piouſly read,& probably belieued
by faithful ſoules for 1400. yeares
ſince, cannot but temerariouſly be
reiected now, and contemned by
Proteſtants; whoſe corrupt Iudgment, as I regard not in this my
tranſlation: ſo I hope good Catholiques will read it with edification and comfort. For it may
well delight them, as it doth me,
to thinke that we haue anciently
had ſuch ſtore of renowned Saintes liuing in our Country, as, be-

ſides this life, *D. Harpsfeld*, the Engliſh Martyrologe, Prudentiall Ballance, *M. Broughton*, and other ancienter hiſtorians do witneſse, though the Names, and liues of the greateſt part of them are only in the booke of life regiſtred, and will in the generall Iudgmēt be gloriouſly reuealed.

That *S. Wenefride* likewiſe, ſhould liue againe, after her head cut off, and do the things which heere are written of her in her Hiſtorie (the chiefe blocke which incredulous Readers perhaps will ſtumble at) is no more hard to be belieued, then that *Lazarus* after he had bene dead, and ſtinking in his graue, ſhould liue agayne, ſit at table with Chriſt, and be Biſhop of Marſills in *France* many yeares after. And if it be obiected

that

that Christ himselfe, did worke
that miracle, able to do all things:
I may well answere, that he promised his owne power, and far
greater wonders then himselfe
had wrought, to be done by his
seruants, extant now in authenticall Histories às certainely since
performed.

Lastly, I intreat my courteous
Reader, for a Conclusion of this
my Preface, to note & mend with
his penne, these ensuing errours
of my Translation, committed in
the printing by strangers, wholy
ignorant of our English tongue.

Faults

Faults escaped in the Printing.

Pag. 24. lin. 7. *dele* that
Pag. 45. lin. 9. where *read* which
Pag. 75. lin. 1. as *read* or
Pag. 82. lin. 9. their *read* his
Pag. 88. lin. 5. *dele* so
Pag. 94. lin. vlt. his *read* this
Pag. 103. lin. 11. *dele* most
Pag. 109. lin. 16. saying *read* said
Pag. 119. lin. vlt. noble Virginity, *read*
   Martyrdome for your Virginity.
Pag. 120. lin. 1. *dele* of your Martyr-
   dome.
Pag. 121. lin. 14. *dele* he
Pag. 128. lin. 5. Charity *read* Clarity
Pag. 146. lin. 16. in, *read* in a suddaine
Pag. 148. lin. 14. and to be, *dele* to
Pag. 165. lin. 3. fall *read* fell
Pag. 173. lin. 10. *Wales,* read that Coun-
   trey.
Pag. 204. lin. 7. streames *read* streame
Pag. 225. lin. 2. hath *read* had
Pag. 251. lin. 9. was *read* he was
Pag. 269. lin. vlt. little *read* so little.

The

The Prayer, and Sequence *of* S. Wenefride, *taken forth of the ancient Miſſall of England, according to the vſe of* SARVM.

Oratio.

OMnipotens ſempiterne Deus, qui beatam Wenefredam Virginitatis præmio decoraſti: fac nos quæſumus eius pia interceſſione, mundi huius blandimenta poſtponere, & cum ipſa perennis gloriæ ſedem obtinere. Per Dominum noſtrum &c.

The Prayer.

ALmighty and everlaſting God, who haſt adorned Bleſſed Wenefride with the reward of Virginity; grant vs we beſeech thee, through her pious interceſſion, to ſet aſide the delights of this world, and obteyne with her, the throne of everlaſting glory. Through our Lord Ieſus Chriſt &c.

SEQVEN-

SEQVENTIA.

Virgo vernans velut Rosa,
  Agni Sponsa speciosa,
Martyr Christi pretiosa,
      Wenefreda floruit.

Ex Britannis oriunda,
Fide firma, spe iocunda,
Actu sancta, mente munda,
      Mundi mendâ caruit.

Hanc occîdit *Carodocus*,
Quem mox sorbet Orci focus,
Qui prauorum extat locus,
      Quo Sathan exuitur.

Huius argumento rei,
Fons ebullit nutu Dei,
Rubricatæ speciei,
      Quo caput præciditur.

Mira multa hic patrantur,
Cæci vident, muti fantur,
Morbi omnes effugantur.
      Cum fide petentium.

Gloriosa *Wenefreda*,
Maris fluctus nobis seda,
Ne fiamus hosti præda,
      Pia fer præsidium: Amen.

The same in old English.

AS a sweete *Rose* in pleasant spring,
Of heauenly Lambe Spouse louely faire
And Martyr deare of Christ our King
S. Wenefrede *did flourish heere.*

Descended well of *Brittish* race,
In *Fayth* now firme, and *Hope* secure,
With workes *Holy*, and *Soule* in *Grace*,
From worldly filth perseuered pure.

This sacred *Mayd* did Cradocke kill,
And him *Hell* swallowed presently,
Where teares in vayne do run downe still
And *Sathan* burnes incessantly.

A *Token* sure of this strang thing,
Bespotted all with blouddy red,
A *Well* by Gods command doth spring
Where *Tyrant* fierce cut off her head.

Heere wöders great Gods hand doth worke
The blind do see, the dumbe do speake,
Diseases which in bodies lurke
Are cured, when *Fayth* is not weake.

O glorious *Virgin* Wenefrede,
To vs the raging sea appease,
And free vs so from *Sathans* dread
That he on vs may neuer seize. Amen.

THE

THE AVTHORS
OWNE PROLOGVE
TO THE LIFE
OF
S. WENEFRIDE.

To the right Reuerend Father, *Guari-*
nus Prior of *Worcester*, *Robert*, his
spirituall Sonne, Prior also vnworthy of *Shrewsbury*, wisheth Grace
to walke vprightly in the way of
Gods Commandements.

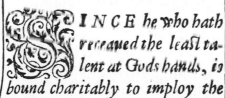

INCE he who hath
receaued the least ta-
lent at Gods hands, is
bound charitably to imploy the

A *same*

same, in the seruice of him who
freely bestowed it, and to the
good of such as may be edified
and benefitted spiritually by it;
not hiding the same vnder a bu-
shell, or reseruing it to himselfe
alone, which will become the
more his owne by being charitably communicated to others in a
holy imitation of our Redeemers bounties, and graces vpon
vs vniuersally bestowed: I haue
iustly feared, out of this respect,
to conceale from others, vnited
in the same band of Christian
Faith, and Charity with me,
and particularly from your

Ve-

Venerable selfe, much respected by me, the Collection which I haue lately made of the Blessed Virgin S. Wenefrides life: the reading whereof, will, I doubt not, help much to increase and perfit heauenly piety, and loue eminently already, and exemplarly to many shining in You; delighted also to dilate the glory of God, & his Saints by workes like to this, which you haue by frequent letters, and earnest intreaties required of me.

I haue gathered the same, partly from the Ancient, and vndoubted Monuments of such

Monasteries, and Churches as this Blessed Virgin is knowne to haue liued in, and partly from the relation of sundry Ancient Priests, for their great learning sanctity of life, and Religious profession, made Venerable, & worthy of all credit, in their assertions, and depositions vnto me.

Three causes haue moued me to publish the true knowledge of this Saints life, so by me attayned vnto. The first, was a wholsome feare (as I haue said) to be reproued by my Eternall Iudge, for hiding vnder groūd,

and

and not imploying profitably as
I ought the talent which he hath
lent me. The second, was my e∫-
peciall loue, and deuotion to this
most renowned Virgin and Mar
tyr of our Countrey, that by her
∫anctity, and great merits heere
by me declared, she might by
faithfull ∫oules be the more deuoutely honoured, ∫erued, and
prayed vnto. The third, was
a particular de∫ire which I haue
charitably had to edifie my owne
Brethren, humbly in their deuo-
tions, and in∫tantly intreating
this labour of me.

 As for S. Wenefrides pre-

tended iourney to Rome, and
other particulars vulgarly only, and by persons of no credit
fabulously reported, I haue wholy omitted them; and forborne
likewise to set downe some other
certaine, and vndoubted relations, concerning her life, because
I would not be tedious, and ouer-
large in my manner of writing:
this which I haue heere gathered
being sufficient, in my opinion,
and yours also I hope, to declare
the eminent sanctity and graces
of this most sacred Virgin, by
whose powerfull intercession,
and your holy prayers, I hope to

re-

receaue, at her heauenly spouses hands, some small reward of my labours, and paynes in this worke vndertaken.

THE

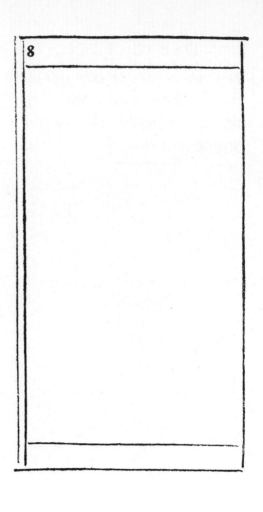

8

THE FIRST BOOKE,
conteyning the History of
S. Wenefrids Life.

CHAPTER I.

Of S. Beuno *his great sanctity ; how he was inspired by God to goe to* S. Wenefrids *Father ; how liberally he was entertayned by him, and had his only child commended for her Education unto him.*

IN the Westerne part of great Britanny, called

A 5   VVales,

VVales, cōioyned Eastwards
in the same continent, with
England, and rounded on all
other sides with *Seuerne*, and
the *Ocean*, flourished in times past innumerable Saintes men and women of sin-
gular sanctity and merit, as
their seuerall Shrines, and
stately Monuments yet re-
mayning do testify; amongst
whome, in King *Eluith* the
second his tyme, one *S. Beuno* was for his wonderfull
graces especially renowned,
who hauing, out of a holy
desire to imitate the pouer-

ty

ty of his heauenly Lord,
and to become a true Pil-
grime heere on earth, forsaken his owne Countrey,
and trodden vnder foote
such glorious pompes, and
pleasures of the world as he
might at home haue en-
ioyed, made himselfe first
a Moncke, and soone after
arriued to such perfection
and sanctity of life, that he
became a common Father
of Religious persons.

For no sooner had he
built a Church and Mona-
stery in one place, and setled
there-

there in regular difcipline
and great purity of life, a
certaine number of Reli-
giõs perfons, but he trauel-
led to another part of the
Countrey, to do there the
like alfo, as Gods holy fpi-
rit for the benefit of many,
peculiarly directed him; fo
that at length he entred into the territory of a rich, &
potent Lord called *Theuith*
fonne to a chiefe Counfel-
lour of the King, & a princi-
pal gouerner of theCoũtry,
who equalled his Illuftrious
birth, by his Noble, Reli-

gious,

gious, & exemplar demea-
nours.

When Venerable *Beuno*
came to this Lords house,
he was most respectfully by
him entertayned, and after
charitable salutatiõs passed
betweene them, the Saint
tould him, that he was sent
by God to erect a Church
in his Territory, as he had
done in other places : and I
doubt not (said he)but that
God hath by a very feruent
and peculiar inspiration,
drawne me hither from his
other seruants, with whome

B li-

I liued els where with great
content, to performe some
great good particularly for
you, and yours . Wherefore
for his diuine Maiesties seruice , I humbly intreate a
small part of your ample
inheritance, to rayse therein a Church, where others
with my selfe will daily pray
for your safety.

The Noble man moued
with the Saintes Venerable
aspect and speaches , resolued forthwith , to graunt
what he asked , and yielded
this wise answere vnto him:

With

Wita good reason, holy Father, am I bound to giue you a part of what Lands I possesse, for the seruice of him, who gaue all vnto me: and I conceaue indeed that you haue pleasured me much, in asking this Charity of me, more profitable to my selfe, then to you. Wherefore this very Mannour which now I liue in, I do from this tyme forward wholy alienate frō my selfe and all myne, yielding the possession, & all right ther of most gladly vnto you:

and

and hauing no more then one child, a tender Virgin, the greateſt delight indeed, and worldly ioy of my hart, I will beſides bequeath her to your holy inſtructions, and prayers, that her life may be holy, and her conuerſation ſuch, as may be pleaſing to God, and contentfull to me alſo.

And hauing put the Saint in poſſeſſion of the place, and promiſed moreouer to help him in the building by him intended, for a conuenient aboad of Gods

Reli-

Religious children and feruants, he chofe afterwards a place for himfelfe to dwell in, vpon a high hill ouer a-gainft it, that when he could not inioy the holy mans prefence, he might a far of looke at leaft towards him, and recreate himfelfe often in the day, by being with him holily and continually imployed in the feruice of God, fpiritually conioyned.

B   CHAP.

CHAP. II.

How S. Wenefrides *Parents did help the Saint in building his Monastery; become also with their Daughter his deuout Auditours and obedient children: How likewise* S. Wenefride *vpon hearing* S. Beuno's *exhortations, resolued to leaue the world, and conserue her virginity, intreating him to mooue also her* Parents *thereunto.*

VV Hen the Saint began to build

his Church and monastery
the Lord *Thewith* did not
faile with meanes liberally
to further it, vouchsafing
also many times to put his
owne hands to this holy
worke for the example of
others, and the sooner to fi-
nish it, as a thing by him
for the glory of God, and
good of his owne scule, exceedingly desired. So as the
Church was no sooner ray-
sed, and made fit for the holy man to preach, and offer
the diuine Sacrifice in, but
himselfe with his Wife and

VVenefride his Daughter, were daily and deuoutely present, at such holy exercises, he obseruing still this Custome to place his Child at the Saintes feete whilst he preached, willing her to be attentiue to his speaches. VVhich became not fruitles in her soule, holily euen then in her tender yeares, and gracioufly prepared feruently to practise in her life, such heauenly documents as from the Saints mouth she continually learned. And her delight in hearing

him

him was such, as with leaue
of her Parents she often visited him alone by her selfe,
to be enriched the more,
with a profitable, and practicall knowledge of diuine
verities from him.

And albeit her Parents,
as their most gracious and
only child, dearely affected
her, and had placed (after
a worldly manner) the only
hope of their posterity in
her, by resoluing with an
ample dowry to marry her
in due tyme, to some No-
ble and chiefe person of the

B 3   Coun-

Country; yet was it a thing most gratefull, and delightfull vnto them, to see her repayre often vnto the Saint, and to season her innocent Soule, as a cleane vessell ordayned by God to contayne afterwards a great measure of heauenly graces, with true piety taught vnto her by him, till at length her heauenly Spouse, by cleare illustrations, and ardent inspirations of his holy spirit, began to worke her sweetly for himselfe, & to make the very thought

of

of a worldly husband; hatefull to her soule, beginning to be ennamored of his owne diuine beauty, and resolued, if she could, by sanctity of life, and her virginity preserued, purely to enioy him.

But now a feare only by her humbly, and dutifully conceaued, of displeasing her Parents, by imparting this her purpose vnto them, troubled her very much, though daily therein more ardently, and vnalterably inflamed; till at length

in this doubtfull conflict,
betweene humane & diuine
loue paffing in her thoghts,
the powerfull Illuminator,
and beft Directour of holy
foules interiourly fuggefted
this counfel vnto her, that
by *Saint Beuno*, whofe holy
fpeaches had occafioned
this pious refolution firft in
her hart firmely then roo-
ted, to propofe it vnto her
Parents, whofe power and
authority she wifely knew
to be very great with them,
by reafon they honoured
him much, and in all things
                        he

he said, gladly obeyed him.
VVherfore one day finding
him alone, after his manner
holily retired, she humbly
and boldly manifested her
purpose thus vnto him.

Holy Father, I come here
to make knowne vnto you
the holy fruites of your
speaches, and Gods graces
togeather in my Soule,
whereby I haue byn effe-
ctually, and (I hope) happily moued to estrange my
selfe wholy from Worldly
contentments, and to con-
secrate my Virginity purely

B 5   to

to him, who liberally gaue
me the beeing I haue , and
hath hitherto cōserued this
enriching Treasure graci-
oufly in me ; Humbly be-
feeching you,to obteyne for
me, my Parents good leaue
and permiffion fo to conti-
nue. The Saint forthwith as
beyond all expreffion de-
lighted to know that the
feedes of diuine grace fowne
by his fpeaches , were beginning to grow fo happily
in her , willingly vnder-
tooke to obteyne of her
Parents what she defired

throgh

throgh the confidence which
he had in their singular piety towards God, & readines
to do what his diuine Maiesty would haue them.

CHAP. III.

S. Beuno *propofeth* S. VVene-
    frides *defire to her Parents,*
    obteyneth their grant therin;
    they giue away in almes her
    intended dowi y, & ioy to fee
    rare beginninges of future
    fanctity, and folide vertues
    in their Daughter.

THe holy mã, a power-
    full Oratour with thẽ

who

who as Children reuerent-
ly respected, and desired to
obey him, in a heauenly
language imparted vnto
them *S. VVenefrids* desires,
and made them withall ca-
pable to know, that it would
be no ordinary act of their
due loue to God, gladly and
freely to dedicate to his seruice what in this world was
dearest vnto them. Their
answere vnto him, with
teares of ioy and praysing
of Christ for his graces affoarded, so singularly, to
their child, was no other

then

then a full, and free leaue
giuen to *S. VVenefride* of
forſaking the world to ſerue
her heauenly Spouſe, who
by ſo high and holy a voca-
tion, had called her vnto
him.

And ſo wishing her a hap-
py progreſſe therein, they
reſolued alſo to draw out of
the ſame this benefitt to
théſelues, that giuing away
to the poore, her ample
dowry for a ſecular mariage
by them prepared, and
diſtributing in holy vſes
beſides, a very great part of

their

their owne princely wealth
and poſſeſsions as trouble-
ſome vnto them, and (with
pouerty delighted) due to
the king of heauen, who by
eſpouſing their Child was
growne to be heyre as it
were vnto them; they might
run more lightly the way of
his commandements, & in
a holy freedome frō worldly ſolicitudes ſpend, & end
the remainder of their life
in gayning to themſelues
heauenly treaſures eternally to enrich them : wherein
they became animated af-

ter-

terwards by the rare example of their daughters vertues; who ouer-ioyed at firſt
with their leaue ſo obtayned,and freed from former
feares of worldly entangle-
ments, daily extended herſelfe to courſes of ſanctity
and perfection by frequent
and feruent practiſes of humility, and punctuall obe-
dience to her holy Father,
permitted by her Parents
freely vnto her.

So as now a corner neere
his Cell where ſhe might
frequently viſit him,and de-

lightfully drawe, through
her eares to her foule, the
vitall breath of his heauenly difcourfes, was in the day
tyme her delightfulleft mã-
fion : and watching whole
nights in the Church, kneeling or proftrate before the
Aultar, when extreme wea-
rines and deadly fleep did
not poffeffe her, was to be as
in her fpoufes bed-chãber,
raifed by amourous thoghts
of his wonderfull Perfe-
ctions, and rapt with pure
delights, freshly euery day
communicated vnto her. So

as

as to heare him only named
caused a iubily in her soule,
by blushing and teares to
such as beheld her sweetely
discouered.

And as internall guists
did wóderfully adorne her;
so were not externall graces
wanting vnto her: for her
face was matchles in bewty
and by a rare modesty ex-
ceedingly graced. Her speach was sweet, neuer but lea-
surely and wisely vttered.
The comly stature likewise
and proportion of her body
in all parts thereof, though

poorely clad serued to grace
her in the eyes of others ; so
as the Diuell emulating
those high beginnings of
sanctity in her , and fearing
withall what her example
might worke in tyme , for
the drawing of others to
like courses of Perfection,
he ceased not to lay many
snares to intrappe her, and
with new temptations ray-
sed by others for her greater
merit & glory at last, incessantly to try her; the beginning of which shall in my
next Chapter be declared.

CHAP.

CHAP. IV.

How S. Wenefride *was found alone by the Kings sonne in her Fathers house; and in daunger to haue byn violated by him, escaped towards the Church, and was in the way cruelly beheaded for constantly refusing to yield her pure body vnto him.*

S. *Beuno* hauing fully ended the fabrique of his Church, and consecrated the same to Christ, was daily

C 2   visi

viſited by great multitudes
of ſuch as dwelled in places
neere him; & amongſt them
S. VVinefreds holy Parents,
neuer fayled in his ſacrifices
and ſermons to heare him;
ſo as on a ſunday whilſt they
were in the Church,& their
daughter by ſome needfull,
or charitable occaſion, contrary to her cuſtome, detai-
ned at home, Prince *Crado-*
cus, king *Alan* his ſonne,with
a luſtful wicked purpoſe entred the houſe, pretending
that he came to ſpeake with
the Lord *Theuith* her Father.

The

The Holy Maid, suspe-
cting no worse of him at
first, after courteous salutatiõs passed betweene them,
and excuses by her humbly
made, of being alone, vn-
attired, and vnable in her
Parents absence fitly to in-
tertayne him as his Princely dignity required, intreated him with all, to repose
himselfe in a more conne-
nient roome of the house,
till after diuine seruice ended, her Father should returne, and be free to speake
with him. To which simple

candor and plainenes of her
speaches gracefully vttered,
the Prince infuriated with
loue of her faire person, and
lustfull desires presently to
inioy her, replyed, that he
would willingly expect the
returne of her Parents, if
herselfe in meane time wold
be pleased to consent vnto
his will, so deuoted vnto her
that for the fauour then ex-
pected from her, he would
according to his Birth, and
Power, euer afterwardes be
ready to honour and serue
her: threatning withall, pre-

sently

sently to rauish her, if she
yielded not willingly to his
motion.

The holy Virgin though
trembling for feare, & blushing at the immodesty of
his speaches, yet lost not her
wits in so needfull an occasion; but present with herselfe, & diuinely also at that
instant assisted, she humbly
and patiétly answered him,
that she doubted not of en-
ioying honour, wealth, and
worldly contentment by being espowsed to so Princely
a person : but because (said

C 4 she)

she) the present poore at-
tire wherein you haue so on
the sodaine taken me, sui-
teth not to so high a mo-
tion, or indeed beseemeth
your presece, giue me leaue,
I beseech you, to enter my
chamber heere by, presently
to alter it.

To which her request (al-
beit with some loathnes to
be delayed in his purpose)
he yielded his consent : so
that she now finding herself
in her chamber, freed out
of his hands, and hopeles of
any rescue or succour to be

other-

otherwise affoarded her, ran
out by a backe way , as fast
as she could , towards the
Church , where her Father
and his people would , she
doubted not, be able to saue
her. But he impatient in his
desires , and suspecting indeed that which happened ,
brake into the roome , and
finding her not there , pursued her so hastely in her
flight, as on a hill side neere
the Church he furiously ap-
prehended her, vowing with
his sword drawne in his
hand, & a countenance full

of wrathful indignation that
if forthwith she confented
not to his will, fo full of ho-
nourable loue towards her,
he wou!d ftrike of that head
from her body, & deforme
that face therein, which formerly he had loued.

W hereunto the holy Vir-
gin (as another. *S. Agnes* to
her carnall Louer) vndaun-
tedly replyed, that she had
holily efpowfed herfelfe, &
that alfo with her Parents
confent, to the king of Hea-
uens fonne, in power, beauty, and goodnes incompara-

bly

bly exceeding him ; and v-
pon his experienced loue
towards her, she would euer
remaine to him so faythfully, constantly, and vnalte-
redly deuoted in the affections of her hart , as she
wold gladly loose her head
and·lite, for refusing to ad-
mit any corriuall togeather
with him . Neither shall
your terrours (said she) or
threats draw me from the
sweetnes of his Loue , or
make me not go, as I haue
promised, purely vnto him.

Whereupon he, in a fu-

rious

rious fcorne to be flighted
fo by her, & knowing withall that whilft she liued the
vehemécy of his loue could
not be affwaged , gaue her
with his fword fo deadly a
ftroake on the neck , as her
head thereby and body be-
came inftantly parted; the
body falling without the
Church dore, and the head
within it ; fo as the floore
therof being fomewhat de-
clining, as built in the han-
ging of a hill , it tumbled
towards the people , kneeling togeather before the

Aultar,

Aultar, aftonishing them with the fight thereof no leffe, thē afterwards it made them worthily to wonder, in feeing a cleere and plentifull fpring newly then beginning to run out of the ground in the fame place, where her head had firft fallen vpon ; vifited fince that time by holy pilgrimes from places farre & neere, and by miraculous graces, and cures frequently affoarded to fickely, and grieued perfons , famoufly renowned .

CHAP.

CHAP. V.

*The lamentations made at S.
Wenefrids death, aswell by
the people as by her Parents;
how likewise S. Beuno pro-
cured by his prayers a dreadfull reuenge of her death v-
pon the Author thereof glo-
rying in his cruelty: and then
putting the head & body togeather, sought to obteyne of
God, her returne to life a-
gaine.*

THE people moued
with so dolefull a spe-
ctacle,

ćtacle, as was the virgins head, bloud, and body, before them, ceafed not with out-cryes to expreffe their griefe and anger togeather towards him that committed fo haynous an outrage. Her Parents likewife called by their cryes to the place, lamented the loffe of their holy fweet child, lying butchered fo villainoufly, and vnexpectedly before them, with more then imaginable expreſsions of forrow.

S. *Beuno* in like manner, now ready to celebrate, lea-

uing the auitar, and approa-
chinge to the doore, was
wholy diſſolued into teares
of compaſſion and griefe to
behold his deare Pupill and
child, lying ſo cruelly murdered, before her conſe-
cration to Chriſt, ſolemnly
ſoone after by him inten-
ded: and beholding in this
his griefe, her Murderer
ſtanding proudly by, & wi-
ping his bloudy ſword on
the graſſe, ſo far from repen-
ting him of the deed, without feare of God or man, as
he gloried proudly therein,

with

with the holy virgins head
in his hand he went towards
him; and looking him in
the face, said vnto him.

Thou wicked man, for
as much, as without re-
gard of innocency or beauty, thou haft murdered a
Princely Virgin, no leffe
noble then thy felfe, and art
not, as thou oughteft to be,
forry afwell for the horrible
facriledge, as foule murder
heere committed deteftably
by thee; I do heere befeech,
my heauenly Lord, for the
example of others at leaft,

D   to

to execute prefently , his dredfull Iudgment againft thee who haft murdered his fpoufe, troubled his people, violated his Saboath, and befprinkled with bloud this holy Houfe, to his honour and feruice confecrated by me .

And the effect of his words , to the terrour and wonder of all prefent, was fuch, as the Prince fell dead fudaynely before him ; and which increafed the afto-nishment of the people, his dead body was prefently ei-

ther

ther swallowed vp by the
earth, or taken away by Di-
uels, so as no signe thereof
afterwards appeared.

This done, *S. Beuno* of-
ten kissing the virgins dead
face, and bathing it with his
teares, put it to her body, &
coueringe them with his
cloake, after he had breathed in her mouth, prepa-
red himselfe to goe to the
Aultar, warning the people
and her Parents especially,
to cease their lamentations,
& conuert thé into prayers
to the Creatour of soules, &

the sole rayser of bodies after death, that he would be
mercifully pleased, as he
called *Lazarus* to a new life
rotten before, and stincking
in his graue; so to rayse this
Princely Spouse heere butchered for her loue towards
him: and this chiefly for the
glory of himselfe, edification of his people, and comfort of her parents, who so
freely before had dedicated
her, in purity of life perpe-
tually to serue him.

CHAP.

CHAP. VI.

How S. Wenefride was ray-
sed from death to life , and
her Head reunited to her bo-
dy by S. Beuno's prayers ,
with a small white circle re-
mayning in the place of her
Necke where it was cut ; &
other wonders gracing stil the
place of her Martyrdome .

AFter the holy mã had
ended his Masse, and
the people their prayers, lif-
ting vp his hands towards
heauen , he prayed in this

manner : O Lord Iesus-
Christ, for whose sake this
holy Virgin contemned the
world, and coueted heauenly things; vouchsafe by the
tender bowels of thy mer-
cy, loue, and bounty, to
graunt vs the effect of our
vowes now made, & prayers
offered heere humbly vnto
thee : and albeit we are fully
persuaded, that this Godly
Virgin who liued holily, &
dyed constantly for thee, be
now highly exalted in heauen also with thee, wanting
no more the society of vs

mor-

mortall & miserable Crea-
tures; yet to manifest thyne
Omnipotency, and that su-
preme dominiō which thou
hast ouer soules and bodies,
neuer dead to thy power of
raysing & reuniting them ;
for the greater merit also of
her soule, whose body heere
lyeth before vs, we craue a
new life for her, and that she
may returne, after a long &
plentifull haruest, of new
merits heere gayned, more
enriched & diuinely beau-
tified vnto thee, the beloued
of her Hart , and Eternall

D 4 spouse,

spouse, who with the Father and the holy Ghost, doest rule in earth, and raigne in heauen, for euer and euer.

And when the people had cryed with great deuotion, *Amen* vnto his prayer, the Virgin as newly wakened from sleep, wiped her eyes & face, besmeared with sweat and dust before, as hauing tumbled on the ground, filling all present, and her Parents there amongst them, with ioy and admiration; obseruing also, as they more fixedly beheld her, a pure

white

white circle, no bigger then a small threed, to remayne in her faire Necke, shewing the place where it had ben cut off before, and was miraculously then to her body conioyned; which because it euer afterwards remayned cóspicuously seene after the same manner, *Brewa*, her name before, is said to haue ben changed by the peoples great veneration, and loue towards her, into *VVenefride* by *VVen*, which doth signify *white* in the old British tongue, added vnto it, & 2.

let-

letters thereof, for better
sound quite altered. And in
many apparitions of her to
men, and women after her
second corporall death, authentically recounted, this
white Circle in her necke
conspicuously appeared; to
giue worldly soules thereby
to vnderstand, the particular glory which she had receaued of her heauély spouse
for suffering that wound, so
constantly for him.

And whereas the valley
where she was martyred,
had ben called euer before a

dry

dry or barren bottome, it was for the Chriftall fountayne of pure waters, breaking miraculoufly out of the ground where her head firft fell, called afterwards in memory of this miracle, *Finhon*, which in old Welfh doth fignify a fountayne or well: & indeed as this fountayne was wonderfull in the firft origen therof, fo did the fame by miraculous cures of men & beafts, either bathed in that water, or drinking therof, become famoufly afterwards, renowned.

In

In memory likewise, that
store of the Virgins pure
bloud had ben spilt in that
place, and to signify withall
how sweet a Sacrifice was offered there by her; the stones of the Well, are either
dyed, or spotted all ouer
with drops, as it were, of
bloud; and the mosse growing about it, is, as with
muske yet to this day sweetly perfumed.

The miracle of her ray-
sing frõ death to life diuulged in those partes, gayned
to *S. Beuno* so great a fame of

his

his singular sanctity, and power with God to obteyne any thing, that multitudes thereupon of Gentil people in those dayes, for their instruction in the Christian fayth and Baptisme, repayred vnto him: whose famous acts, and *S. VVenefrids* holy life after her being raysed, shall in the rest of this booke be briefly declared.

CHAP.

CHAP. VII.

How S. Wenefride was so-
lemnly veyled by S. Beuno,
and fully instructed in the
true knowledge & holy pra-
ctise of a Religious life. How
likewise he tooke his leaue af-
terwards of her, propheti-
cally fortelling the sanctity
of her life, and her gayning
to Christ of many soules.

S. *VVenefride*, as another
Lazarus restored to a
new life, with a fresh feruour of heauenly loue and

deuo-

deuotion, applyed herselfe
to learne from so great a
maister as *S. Beuno* was, how
to rayse her already-illumi-
nated soule to the height of
Religious Perfection, choo-
sing for that purpose to sit
at the Saints feet, as *S. Mary
Magdalen* did at the feet of
our Sauiour, neuer satiated
with the delicacies, which
fell from that heauenly Table vnto her, by his most
pious speaches, and deuout
instructiós; & within a smal
tyme out a restles and most
amorous desire, fully to be

vni-

vnited to her louely and diuine Spouſe, she obteyned
of him (as profeſſed Virgins were wont to be, in
thoſe primitiue tymes of
Gods church) to be ſolénly
veiled, her ſingular vertues
& graces ſupplying the wāt
of yeares, for that Religious
ceremony Canonically re-
quired.

The Saint therefore de-
ſirous to affoard her that
comfort, and knowing her
to be very worthy therof,
called her Paréts vnto him,
to acquaint them with his

intent

intent of giuing vnto her
the holy veyle of Chaſtity
with their approbation and
conſent: which they, as deuout & godly perſons, with
all humble reſpects vnto
him the Author of her ſe-
cond life, and with imbra-
cings of their holy Child,
moſt gladly agreed vnto;
& which was afterwards in a
great aſſembly of people
moſt ſolemnely, and reli-
giouſly performed.

After which bleſſing by
her obteyned, the holy man
as diuinely foreknowing, to

E   what

what an height, of sanctity &
perfection the spirit of god,
for the glory of himselfe &
good of others, intended to
raise her, sought more and
more to illuminate her soule
by heauenly documents, &
practicall lessons, for the direction of herselfe, & others
in a spirituall and Religious
life; which she as a very apt
scholler did not only learne,
but practise also in such a
manner, that the Saint was
ouerioyed to behould her.

And finally finding her
fully enabled not only to

guide

guide herſelfe, but others alſo, in courſes of Perfection ,
he called her Parents one
day vnto him, and tould
them, that as they had liberally graunted vnto him a
Church, and houſe for the
ſeruice of God, and help of
his ſeruants: ſo had his diuine Maieſty liberally re-
quited their Charity to-
wards him, by ſingular graces affoarded to them, and
eſpecially to their Childe,
whom now they might well
chooſe, and propoſe vnto
themſelues, as a Miſtreſſe

able to guide them in their
Redeemers seruice, and as
a bright shining patterne of
religious Perfection. Wherfore being diuinely called
to another plaee, I muſt
heere (ſaid he) leaue you
to the helpes of Heauenly
Graces, which will not be
wanting vnto you, perſi-
ſting as now you do holily
in Gods ſeruice, and to the
carefull direction of your
Daughter.

And then, conuerting
himſelfe to *S. VVenefride*:
Our Lord (ſaid he) deare

Child,

Child, hath appointed you
to succeed me heere in my
holy labours, and abiding in
these parts, to go onwards
happily your self, & to guide
others fruitfully, in the way
to eternall life, as hitherto
I haue taught you . And
doubt not, but by the mo-
uing example of your death
for him already susteyned,
and the holy conuersation
of your life, you wilbe able
to performe what I haue
said; and in this very place,
gather togeather for your
heauenly spouse, many pure

E 3   and

and deuout Virgins, guided
vnto him holily by you.

But know withall, that
you shal not heere end your
dayes, but that after seauen
yeares, in prayer and pen-
nance spent in this place, to
your owne great Merit,
& singular edification of o-
thers, our gracious Lord
will call you to another,
that strangers also may in
the knowledge and true seruice of him be illuminated
by you: and know also that
heerby your memory shall
become glorious in future

ages,

ages, and your merits published to the whole world, by
miraculous cures, & helpes
affoarded vnto sickly, and
distressed persons praying
vnto you.

E 4   CHAP.

CHAP. VIII.

VVherein is declared S. Wenefrides *griefe for her Holy
Fathers departure*, *and his
comfortable speaches* ᴠnto
her, *concerning particular
Graces intended by God towards herselfe*, *and others by
her*.

THe Godly Virgin be-
ing excessiuely grie-
ued at her holy Fathers departure, he to cõfort her in
so deep an affliction, tooke
her by the right hand, and
lead

lead her to the fountayne
which miraculoufly had ri-
fen in the tyme, & place of
her martyrdome, & fitting
togeather vpō a ftone neere
to the fide of the well, called
therefore to this day *S. Beuno's* ftone. You fee (faid he)
heere the monumēt of your
fufferings, and behold alfo
the ftones therein fteyned
as with your bloud, shed
for your Heauenly Spoufes
fake; be you therfore now
attentiue, and mindfull of
what I shall fore-tell you
concerning three efpeciall

Graces, whereby your Glorious spouse Christ Iesus wil heerafter honour your selfe, and benefit others by you.

The first of them is, that these said Stones, shall neuer be washed from their bloudy steynes, but euer retayne the same, as triumphant signes, and glorious testimonies of your bloud, in defence of your Chastity most gratefully heere effused.

The second shalbe, that neuer any person who shall deuoutely aske any

tempo-

temporall blessing, as free-
dom aswell from corporall
as spirituall distresses, to be
obteyned by your merits &
prayers for them, but that
in three times so doing they
shall assuredly be made par-
takers of their desire, or passing by death out of this
life, they shall in another
world reap after a more ample manner the fruit of their
prayers, by heauenly blessings, through your inter-
cessions for them, diuinely
prepared.

The third shalbe, that after

ter my departure now from
you, into a remote part of
this Iland, God will giue me
a Cell neere the sea shore, &
when you would send any
letters, or tokens vnto me
(as his diuine Maiesty wold
haue you to do, and I also
do intreate the same of you
once at least euery year)cast
them only in the streame of
this fountayne, and they
will, passing into the Ocean
by many creekes, and tur-
ning-shores, be diuinely, &
safely directed vnto me :
which graces likewise to the

worlds

worlds end shall be diuulged glorieufly of you.

And hauing ended this
his fpeach, he led her backe
againe vnto the Church,
and faid then vnto her : Behould heere this Church,
& lodgings about it, which
hauing byn built by the
charitable magnificence of
your parents , and my la-
bours, I leaue vnto you, to
be conuerted into a copious
monaflery of Chaft, & De-
uout Virgins , who moued
by your inftruction , & holy example of life, shall to-

gea-

geather with your selfe, me-
ritoriously practise those
heauenly documéts, which,
by a perfit contempt of the
world, and a full abnegation
of théselues (the two maine
grounds of Religious perfection) I haue often deliuered
by my speaches vnto you.

Stupendious miracles al-
so done for the temporall &
eternall good of many, repayring to this very place,
shall heerafter be effected,
to the prayse of their heauenly Maker , and euen
bruit beasts shall not want
their

their share in such blessings; striue therfore, deare Child to exhibit your selfe in all things, as a liuely patterne, and example to others of all Vertue. As for my poore selfe, I shall goe whither Gods spirit will guide me, & euer retayne in my hart and soule, a Fatherly and louing memory of you.

CHAP.

CHAP. IX.

Of the continuance of S. Wenefrides *griefe for the departure of* S. Beuno ; *and how
he tooke lastly his leaue of
her.* VVho *beginning afterwards to practise what he
had taught her, gathered many Noble mens daughters vnto her, and liued in eminent
sanctity , as Gouernesse of
the rest .*

THE more *S. Beuno*
did seeke by sweete
speaches to comfort his louing

louing Child, the more was her griefe for his abſence in-creaſed, eſpecially when she ſaw him with his ſtaffe in his hand ready to go from her, ſweetly venting her ſorrows in ſuch ſort as others might heare her , ſpeaking thus vnto him .

Now holy Father am I to be lelft alone, as a poore Orphane Child without a Nurſe, or as a ſilly sheep a-mõg rauenous wolues with-out a Paſtour to defend me; wheras with you I was moſt ſafe, alwayes ioyfull in your

F   pre-

presence, alwayes edified by your example, & instructed by your speaches. Which words of hers, together with her flowing teares so moued the Saint himselfe, as also her louing Parents, and others that were present, as not to haue their owne sorrow, by staying longer with her, increased, after he had blessed her with his hand, (as hauing no toūg through griefe to speake a word more vnto her) hastned his pace faster then modesty would permit her to follow him,

vntill

vntill at length he was gon
quite out of her sight, neuer
more in this world to be
hold him; so that returning
with her companiõs home-
ward, for many dayes after
she remayned in her sor-
row, till tyme at length, &
discret thoughts hauing eased her hart, she wisely and
maturely, began to reflect
vpon his heauenly discour-
ses and lessons formerly giuen vnto her, both how she
might practise them her-
selfe, and draw others also to
the exercise therof.

Which in a short tyme,
Gods grace and the force of
her holy Example, did so
happily effect, that a great
number of Noble and de-
uout Virgins, trampling
worldly wealth, Honours &
pleasures vnder their feet,
for the glory and seruice of
Christ, betooke themselues
to her gouernment, & liued
in religious discipline holily vnder her; commanding
or teaching them nothing
but what herselfe practised
first amongst them, as a shining cleere Light, in safe

paths

paths of sanctity, to guide
them; yea with such a sweet
mildenes , & motherly loue
towards them , that with e-
quall merit , and contentment they obeyed her com-
mands, and obserued such
rules as she had established
amongst them.

Her wholsome aduises al-
so they receaued as heauēly
oracles; & such remedies as
in their difficulties, & temptations she wisely & com-
passionably gaue them, had
a heauenly kind of force
presently to free them . Mi-

racies likewise were not
sometymes wanting to in-
creafe her authority, and to
testify her sanctity vnto
them; so that their respect
and loue towards her, caused all to striue who should
excell in imitating the rare
vertues, which daily more
and more they discouered
in her holy example of life,
beeing as a sweet odour,
wherby perfect soules come
to draw others vnto Christ
with them.

CHAP.

CHAP. X.

Of the Fame, and effects of S. *Wenefrides sanctity of life in numbers of soules gayned vnto Christ by her. Of the first guift also which she sent miraculously to* S. Beuno.

THE wonderfull fame of *S. VVenefrids* sanctity, increased also by miraculous cures, vpon persons diseased done frequently & apparently by her, was not contayned within the limits only of the country where

F 4   she

she dwelt, but far and neere
againft her will, began to be
fo diuulged, from very re-
moteplaces of the kingdom;
fo as many flocked to fee, &
fpeake with her, and were fo
edified by her Angelicall
behauiour, & wife fpeaches
vnto them, that they were
very loath to leaue her cōpany, and accounted thofe
people bleffed who liued,
alwayes neere her.

But moft of all the holy
Virgins that were placed
vnder her care, & domeftical
gouerment, reputed them-

selues happy, by hauing for
their Guide, no lesse tender a Mother in her deare
loue towards them, then a
wise mistresse by instruction
and example holily to di-
rect them, as her holy Father had formerly taught
her; towards whome during
her life, she euer retayned
a most gratefull memory of
her present life, and a thou-
sand blessings besides receaued from him. In particular
also she forgot not the yearely token she had promi-
sed to send him.

F 5   Where-

Wherefore partly with her owne hands, and partly by the help of her fifters, fhe had imbrodered a faire veftemēt to fend vnto him, and hauing in the beginning of the month of May, almoft a yeare after his departure, finifhed the fame, wrapping it vp in a wollen cloath, fhe went with her fifters, & many others to the welsfide, where cafting it into the water, fhe faid; O holy Father I fend heere according to your command & my promife, this fmal token

of

of my loue vnto you.

The which , to the great
wőder of many viewing the
fame, as it paffed by the well
ftreame downe into the Ri-
uer , and fo into the fea, remayned dry , and no whit
moiftned by the water : So
that in a short tyme , being
diuinely directed, it was caft
on the shoare 50. miles off
hard by the Monaftery ,
where the holy man liued,
and he cafually going forth
tooke it vp, wődring at firft
what it should be , till at
length opening the bundle

and

and remébring his charge
giuen to *S·VVenefride* before
his departure, he ioyfully
conceaued it to be her guift,
gratefully mindfull of his
loue towards her; and ioyed
therein much more after-
wards, when the wonderfull
sanctity, and fruites of her
life were reuealed vnto him;
as she also diuinely knew
that he had safely recea-
ued it.

The vestment he orday-
ned to be kept carefully in
the Church, for the vse of
himselfe and his Brethren,

to

to celebrate holy maſſe in ;
& renuing often by the ſight
therof, his wonted loue and
prayers for her , he became
in them illuminated againe,
and prophetically aſſured,
that her owne graces should
be eminent , and the fruites
very great which by her holy life, & exáple to the glory
of God, & good of others,
should be wrought , both
where she liued, and in many other places, as formerly
he had byn inſpired to tell
her .

CHAP.

CHAP. XI.

*Of the great Talents which
Christ gaue vnto S. Wene-
fride for the good of others ;
and how she yearely remem-
bred to send her token to S.
Beuno, vntill, to her great
griefe , she had his holy end
reuealed vnto her ; soone
after which, she changed the
place of her aboad, as he had
foretold her .*

Albeit many Graces
were worthily admi-
red in his holy Virgin, by
those

thofe who knew, and con-
uerfed with her, as her high
& lasting vnion with God
in extaticall prayer , her
great austerity , her Angelicall purity and innocency
of life, her powerfull authority in commanding her
fubiects, with admirable humility and fweetnes conioyned; yet nothing was more
wonderfull in her, then the
deep knowledge of heauen-
ly verityes, and ardent zeale
of her Creatours glory, still
manifested in her exhorta-
tiõs to her owne fubiects, &

fpeaches

ſpeaches to ſtrangers that
came to viſit her; ſo as ſhe
did fill their harts more
with enflamed deſires to
ſerue Almighty God, then
their eares with the ſound
of her wordes : euer attri-
buting the graces of her
ſoule firſt to Chriſt, & next
to *S. Beuno* his Great ſeruát
and her Teacher, to whome
ſhe euery yeare ſent her
promiſed token, or preſent
after the manner aforeſaid,
vntill his holy death, and
circumſtances thereof were
reuealed vnto her; whoſe

loſſe she frequently afterwards deplored, albeit she
had ben diuinely aſſured,
that according to his wonderfull merits heere on
earth, he was in heauenly
ioyes, highly exalted: the
particulars of whoſe holy
life from his Childhood till
his death, and great miracles afterwards, are authentically recorded in his yet
extant and certaine monu-
ments.

After whoſe glorious diſ-
ceaſe, she began to feele
moſt perfect deſires in her-

G   ſelfe,

selfe, for the greater glory of
God and benefit of soules
in other places, to remoue
from the monastery where
she liued, especially now
seeing her sisters well able
to liue holily & religiously
without her. So that in the
end of the seauenth yeare of
her gouerment, as the Saint
had foretold her, she tooke
leaue of her spirituall Children, Parentes, and other
friends there abouts, all af-
flicted aboue measure, at
the losse of her gratefull, &
profitable presence amongst
them;

them; and togeather with one of her companions intended to goe whither the spirit of God should be pleased to direct her: visiting also deuoutly before her departure, the place of her owne martyrdome, & there prostrate on her knees, in húble & feruent prayer she besought Almighty God, that he would according to his blessed will, direct her in that iourney for his honour intended, and to increase withall his blessings vpon such as frequented

G 2   that

that place, in a deuout memory of her martyrdome
there for him sufteyned;the
which effect of her prayer
was by his diuine Maiefty
accordingly graúted as hath
ben teftified fince by num-
berlefse miracles wrought
at that Well, or Fountaine,
in curing the bodily & fpi-
rituall infirmities of all hū-
ble Clients and fuppliants
in that place vnto her.

CHAP.

CHAP. XII.

How S. Wenefrid *was directed by God in her iourney to a holy mã called* Deifer, *whose Counsell she was willed to follow: of whom many things are by the Author occasional-ly heere recounted; and how worthy he was to be chosen by God, for* S. Wenefrides *Directour in the place of* S. Beuno.

S. *VVenefride* haning in earnest prayer recom-méded her iourney to God, was inspired to goe with her companion, to one *Deifer* a holy Man, liuing at *Bota-uar*, who should further direct her. This man was indeed, for his Sanctity in those dayes, & miraculous testimonies therof, famously renowned ; for by his prayers he had raised out of the ground a goodly spring in a place that was dry before, & obteyned likewise of God, that the water thereof should haue a supernaturall force to cure all soares & diseases of such as did drinke

ther-

therof, or wash their ſoares
therewith .

And amongſt many mi-
racles beſides recounted of
him whilſt he liued, this one
performed after his death
is eſpecially renowned, to
wit, of two Theeues who hauing ſtolne two horſes out
of his Churchyard, poſted
with them moſt ſpeedily out
of the Coūtrey: but the next
day the owners finding thē
gone , humbly proſtrated
themſelues before the Saintes Aultar, and preſented
therat two Candels for the

recouery of their horses, beseeching him to accept of
thé vnlighted as they were,
since they had no fire there
present to kindle them.

This faithfull piety of
theirs so pleased the Saint,
that the Candels were vp-
on the suddayne miracu-
loufly lighted to testify that
he gracioufly heard them: &
the theeues after they had
ridde their horses as they
thought far from the place
found themselues brought
backe againe vnto it, & that
not once but the second

tyme

tyme alſo ; ſo as the men hauing prayed there all night,
early in the morning as they
came out of the Church,
they very ioyfully ſaw their
horſes, held by two ſtrangers wholy confounded at
their theft : wherfore they
gladly ſeizing on them, &
humbly thanking the Saint
by whoſe merits they had
obteyned that bleſſing, they
diſmiſſed alſo the theeues
for his ſake, without infli-
ting any punishment (as
their fault deſerued) vpon
them. Which miracle I haue

purposely heere recounted, that my Reader may know the merits & great sanctity of blessed *Deifer*, to whom *S. VVenefride*, for the knowledge of her iourney, was diuinely directed.

CHAP.

CHAP. XIII.

How S. Wenefride *came to the Holy man* Deifer *, and after she had bin charitably welcommed, and entertayned by him for one night, she was the next morning sent, for a further direction, to another Saint called* Saturnus, *dwelling at* Henthlant.

THe holy Virgin after due inquiry made, where the Village *Botauar* ſtood, and of her way vnto it, committing to God her

mona-

Monastery at *Finhon*, and
friends there about, began
with her companion chere-
fully her iourney towards
Blessed *Deifers* Cell, eight
miles distant; where at her
arriuall, she was by the
Saint charitably welcom-
med; and hauing related the
cause of her comming, and
how she had byn diuinely in
her prayer, directed vnto
him, he tould her that concerning either herselfe, or
her iourney, God had not as
then reuealed any thing vnto him : But haue patience

(said

(said he) a little this night, to stay heere at my cell, and his diuine maiesty the whilst will vouchsafe perchance to reueale his holy pleasure vnto me.

Whereunto she humbly and thankefully agreed, as being confidently assured, that Almighty God had not vainely, and to no purpose, directed her vnto him.

The Saint, as his manner was, praying the whole night, a heauenly voyce towards the morning saying thus vnto him; Tell *VVene-*
fride

fride my Virginall deare Daughter , that she goe forthwith to a village called *Henthlant* where she shall be partly satisfyed in her desire, for there she shal find a Venerable man called *Saturnus* , by whome she shall be more fully instructed, about the place of her aboad during life , and what she shall do in it .

So that early in the morning *S. Deifer* calling the holy Virgin his guest , concealed nothing of what had ben reuealed vnto him, and

dire-

directing her the way towards *Saturnus* his Cell, willed her cheerefully to goe on; for that holy neighbour of mine (said he) will be diuinely enabled to tell you, not only of your iourney, and place to goe vnto, but of other things also, belonging to you.

CHAP.

CHAP. XIV.

How Saturnus *entertayned* S.
Wenefride *in his Cell , and
telling her , how much God
should be honoured by her , he
directed her to a holy place
called* Guitherin , *where
she should find one* Elerius,
*a Blessed Abbot of religious
men to direct her , and a monastery of chast Virgins, who
would gladly submit themselues vnto her.*

S. *VVenefride* much reioy-
cing   at   the   direction

which

which Blessed *Deifer* had giuen her, and confirmed in her comfortable persuasion that Christ the Author of her iourney, would not in his care and protection be wanting vnto her, humbly and thanckfully tooke her leaue of him, and went on forwards with her companiō towards *Henthlant* where *Saturnus* remayned.

Comming thither she was most charitably receaued by him, as hauing bin, concerning herselfe and her iourney, before hand diui_

H   nely

nely inftructed; and caufing
her to remayne that night
in prayer, and holy conferences with him, he gaue
vnto her (to her great com
fort) many heauenly & holy leffons, and towards the
morning he tould her, that
their was a place, not far off
called *Guitherin*, ftored with
the pretious reliques of many Saints who had formerly
liued there, in great holines
of life, and deerenes vnto
God, bleffing the place for
them ; and for that caufe
greatly reuerenced by de-
uout

uout people repayring vn-
to it. This place (said he) is
deſtined by God for your
earthly habitation, and to
be ſanctified more by you ;
where alſo you shall find a
holy Abbot called *Elerius*,
of ſo great mortification,
prayer, & vnion with God,
as the world, and all con-
rentments therof are who-
ly dead vnto him.

To this Man then am I
willed to ſend you, and to
tell you with all, that you
shall find there a heauenly
tranquillity of mind, and a

Monaſtery of chaſt Virgins, trayned vp from their Infancy in vertue, liuing alſo now holily togeather, yet ordeyned by God to be rayſed by your holy Example and Inſtructions to higher and perfecter wayes of gayning ſanctity and religious perfection; and they will in time, for that end, humbly and gladly be ready to ſubmit themſelues vnto you, as to a Mother and Abbeſſe, ſent by their Heauenly ſpouſe purpoſly vnto them.

CHAP.

CHAP. XV.

How S. Wenefride *going to*
Elerius *, was in the way ,*
faluted moſt charitably by
him ; how alſo after they had
ſpent a whole night in prayer
togeather , ſhe was led by him
to the monaſtery of Virgins,
and there after high prayſes
vttered of her ,ſhe was com-
mended as a companion diui-
nely ſent vnto them.

S. *VVenefride* replenished
with incredible ioy at
Saturnus ſpeaches vnto her,

H 3   eſpe-

especially in hearing how holy a place she was going vnto, and that she should find there a Monastery of chast virgins to liue withal, desired to know of him the way thitherward, crauing withall his holy blessing for the better speed of her iourney.

The Holy man, guiding her himselfe some part of the way, for the great reuerence he bare towards her, after he had giuen her his blessing, caused his Deacon to accompany her through-

out

out the whole iourney to
Elerius, who being diuinely
forewarned of her com
ming, and all other particulars of her life, met her for
honours fake vpon the way,
and after he had led her into the Church, and prayed
a while with her, he imbraced her in a fatherly louing
manner, bidding her be of
good comfort : for, faid he,
(taking her a part from the
Deacon, and her Compa
nion) I haue already diui
nely vnderſtood of your
noble Virginity, with other

H 4   grace-

gracefull signes of your martyrdome, in the place thereof yet remayning, and will be gladly ready to help you, in the cause of your iourney vnto me.

Whereunto *S. VVenefride* replyed, that she had nothing more concerning herselfe to tell him, but that as she had ben by Gods holy spirit guided vnto him, so would she be hūbly ready to receaue his further directions, and be in the future course of her life an obedient Child, and Schol-

ler

ler vnto him.

The Saint by this her humble and modeſt anſwere being exceedingly edified, tould her, that they would if she pleaſed, ſpend that night in holy prayer togeather, for their ſurer direction, in ſo important an occaſion: and he hauing receaued towards the morning, new illuminatiõs from heauen about her, replenished with exceſſiue ioy, he roſe from his prayer, and hartily imbracing her, willed her to be confident, that God

H 5   would

would not be wanting in the
wonted effects, and gracious
increasing of his Fatherly
loue towards her; & so lea-
ding her out of the Church
to the Monastery of Vir-
gins gouerned by him,
he made this speach vnto
them.

Deare Children of God,
reioyce, for that your heauenly spouse hath sent a new
star of wonderful brightnes
to shine heere among you,
& prouided such a compa-
niõ for you, as wil with new
treasures of merited graces

enrich

enrich her owne soule, and
yours also by the many rare
examples, and high practises of religious Perfection,
which from tyme to tyme
she will exhibit profitably,
and holily vnto you.

For this is *VVenefride* that
renowned Virgin , whome
you haue heard to haue suf-
fered a glorious death , for
her virginity deféded. This
is she, whose Triumphs are
sung in Churches , and her
Trophies do yet illustrate
the whole Prouince which
she dwelled in . This is she
who

who in her martyrdom and Confeſſion , is equally glorious , and now is come to liue holily, and to dye happily amongſt you,as hauing already a high place amōgſt the moſt glorious Martyrs of heauen reſerued for her.

Reioyce therefore worthily at her fortunate arriuall, and keep ſafely ſo heauenly a Treaſure amongſt you. Marke well and imitate diligently the rare example of her life: forget not likewiſe thoſe heauenly leſſons which ſhe will giue you, out

of

of a holy defire , to leade
you, with herfelfe vnto the
height of religious merit &
perfection; for which only
reafon Chrift hath fent her
to increafe alfo the already renowned glory of this
place , by liuing heere a-
mongft you .

CHAP.

CHAP. XVI.

Of the commendation which the Saint made of S. Wenefride *to the old Abbeſſe of the Monaſtery; and how she quickly there deſerued his prayſes by her eminent, and heroicall Vertues.*

S. *Elerius* hauing ſpoken ſo much of her ſanctity generally to all the ſiſters of the Monaſtery togeather, conuerted his ſpeach vnto the Venerable old Abbeſſe called *Theonia,* a very holy

wo-

woman, saying thus vnto her.

To you, most deare Mother, I recommend especially the respectfull entertaynement of this sacred and deare spouse of Christ, sent (as I say once againe) diuinely vnto you, wherby you may gather how highly she is to be honored by you; & ioy withall that the Author of all graces hath in sending her hither so louingly regarded you: & with this he departed, leauing *S. VVenefrid* amongst them, who suitably

to

to his high prayſes, began to shine in her wonderfull perfections, and by heroi-call acts of vertue to infuſe a new Charity amongſt thé, eaſily by all diſcerned,& by the Abbeſſe eſpecially,who was no raw beginner in re-gular and holy courſes.

Her abſtinence (they no-ted) was admirable , her prayer cótinuall when cha-ritable occaſions interrup-ted not the ſame,& very of-ten extaticall; a profound Humility in all her geſtures and ſpeaches plainely ap-

peared,

peared, neuer prayfing herfelfe, and fenfibly troubled
when others for any thing
did extoll her. Patience the
firft fruite of Charity, as *S.*
Paul reckoneth it, feemed to
haue poffeffed fo fully her
hart, and fo firmely fetled
the affections thereof, as all
Anger, Enuy, and other dif-
ordinate Paffions of that
kind were wholy dead vnto
her.

Her Commands had euer
fuch fweetnes and difcretion
conioyned, as it delighted
all the other to do whatfoe-

uer she, at *Theonia's* intreaty
commanded them, especial-
ly when they noted herselfe
in hard offices to goe before
them . And when she spake
either of sacred Verities or
of vertuous Practises vnto
them, the feeling feruour of
diuine loue flamed not only
in her soule , but a great
depth of heauély wisedome
appeared plainely in her
words also , & wrought the
like effects in such as heard
them ; so as Reuerence and
Loue were quickly by all
yielded vnto her.

Theo-

Theonia the Abbesse also as more illuminated, to know, and delight in her graces, did often confer priuately with her, alwayes learning at such tymes new lessons of sanctity from her. And seldome did they so conferre togeather of sacred Misteryes, Ioyfull, or Dolorous, but that both their harts, with loue and compassion equally possessed, caused teares to flow frō their eyes in aboundance, and their loud sobbings to interrupt their discourse; so as the one

I 2   ioyed

ioyed in her deuout ſcholler
and the other was no leſſe
pleaſed in hauing ſuch a Miſtreſſe, ſo diuinely prepared
by Chriſt, for her.

CHAP.

CHAP. XVII.

How S. Elerius *experiencing* S. Wenefrids *great wisedome and Vertue in many conferences with her, preached her sanctity to his Brethren; And of the many people, who moued with the fame of her Martyrdome and holy life, came from places farre and neere, to see, and speake with her .*

S. *Elerius* liuing with his Monks, not far off, in a most retired, austere and deuout manner, delighted many tymes to visit the holy Virgin in her Monastery, discoursing of heauenly misteries and vertuous Practises with her; and found her so cleerely illuminated in the one, & so solidly grounded in the other, that hauing admired her himselfe, and returning home to his brethren was wont to vtter wonderfull prayses of her vnto them.

And her fame at length by the mouths of many became so diuulged, as from

places

places far & neere, infinite
numbers of all sortes of
people flocked vnto her,
some to know, and see so noble, louely, and holy a Virgin, who had lost her head
to saue her virginity, and after death for her Spouses
greater honour had ben by
a holy Man miraculously
raysed to life , accounting
the place and company she
liued in, most blessed by her
presence : Others, by their
great importunity and earnest prayers obteyned to see
the white pure circle stil re-

mayning in her necke, de-
noting the wound which in
her martyrdome she recea-
ued; the fight whereof caufed them to shed many
teares of loue, and ioy that
Chrift had triumphed fo
glorioufly in her firft, and
fent her afterwards fo happily vnto them.

S.VVenefrid herfelfe would
gladly out of her great and
profoūd humility haue de-
nyed them that fauour; but
a charitable defire of their
good, gayned many wayes
thereby, and the other Vir-

gins

gins intreaties , made her
willing to affoard that contentment vnto them, as fearing not be made proude
with their exceſſiue prayſes,
or apt to aſſume vnto herſelfe any merit , of being ſo
prayſed; the high knowledge indeed which ſhe had of
Gods attributes and perfections , compared with her
owne fraylties and nothing,
being two ſure grounds of
ſolid humility in her.

CHAP.

CHAP. XVIII.

How S. Wenefride *propheti-*
cally foretold in order, the
death of Theonia *firſt ;*
next her owne; and laſtly the
holy end of Elerius *: How*
alſo after the death of Theonia, *ſhe was made Abbeſſe*
by Elerius, *and gouerned*
that Monaſtery in all ſancti-
mony, till her dying day.

Bleſſed *Elerius* viſiting
on a tyme *S. VVenefrid*
in her Monaſtery, to con-
ferre, as his cuſtome was, of

holy

holy things, tould her, speaking occasionaly of the happines to dye well, that he had often reioyced to thinke, that he should haue her neere him at his death, and afterwards to pray for him. No Father (said she prophetically vnto him) it will not fall out so, Christ hauing ordayned the contrary.

For first, you shall liue to bury holy *Theonia* our deare Mother, and me also some few yeares after; which done, you shall in short

tyme

time end holily your dayes,
& paſſe full of merits heere
gayned, to ioyes euerlaſting.

All which proued true,
for very ſoone after *Theonia*
fell into a daungerous ſick-
nes , and finding her ſelfe
neere her end, to comfort
theReligious praying about
her, and bitterly lamenting
her departure from them :
Children (ſaid ſhe) teares
ſhould not be ſhed for friends, or for our ſelues, vnles
ſome euil had hapned to thé
or vs; but in my caſe & yours
the contrary now appeareth

for

for I shall by death, hasten
I hope, to my Heauenly
spouse calling me vnto him;
and you in my place shall
haue blessed *VVenefride*, a
much more holy Mother,
by her good exáple & hea-
uenly instructions to guide
you. Looke vpon her ther-
fore as on a bright starre, &
shining patterne of all vertue; tread the steps, and goe
not out of those holy wayes
wherein she will lead you,
to Religious perfection.

After which words, she
receaued the holy sacramét

at

at Blessed *Elerius* his hands for her *viaticum* towards heauen, & breathed out her pure, and holy soule, gloriously by Angels accompanied thither. After whose exequies solemnly and deuoutly performed, holy *Elerius* ordayned *S. VVenefride* Abbesse in her place, to gouerne the Monastery, which she, in her humility, for a tyme resisted, till Obediéce to the Saint, and Charity to the sisters instantly beseeching her to vndertake the charge, preuayled with her.

No

No sooner was this Office thus imposed on her, but she, like a Candle set on a candlesticke higher then before, began to cast out more brightly her cleere rayes of Vertues, and to giue a new light & life, as it were to the whole Monastery, by her heauenly speaches & examples; so as her humility by the dignity of her Office, with her Patience, Charity, and other Vertues, though admirable before, seemed now to haue ben very much increased in her.

CHAP.

CHAP. XIX.

Of the high esteeme that S. E-
lerius *himselfe*, *with other
Religious*, *and secular Persons made of* S. Wenefride:
*And of the miracles which
she wrought in her Mona-
stery, by curing all sorts of
distressed, or sicke people repayring vnto her.*

S. VVenefride had not li-
ued long Abbesse of the
Monastery, before the fame
of her sanctity & wisedome
came to be, throughout that

whole

whole prouince, fo vniuer-
fally diuulged, as Principall
perfons both of the Clergy
& Laity repayred frequently vnto her, neuer departing
without fingular edifica-
tion, by her behauiour and
fpeaches. Yea euen theeues,
& robbers themfelues, with
other notorious Malefa-
ctours, by her gracious af-
pect and effectuall exhortations made charitably vnto
them, were from their euill
wayes, oftentimes reclay-
med. And now, not only
in priuate houfes, but in

K   Chur-

Churches and pulpits alſo,
were her vertues frequently
recounted, and eſpecially
by *S. Elerius*, beſt acquain-
ted with them, who vſed to
tell his owne diſciples, and
others alſo, that ſhe was diuinely ſent by God, to honour, and benefit the place
& Coũtry where ſhe liued:
and his words proued true,
for no day paſsed almoſt,
wherein her diuine Spouſe,
to ſhew her dearenes vnto
him, did not comfort, and
cure in ſudaine, and miraculous manner, grieued,

ſickly,

fickly, and diftreffed perfons, by the help of her
prayers; fo as her Monaftery was now become a com-
mon refuge vnto them. But
amongft other graces emi-
nent in her, she was noted
to haue had a fingular talent in difcouering temptations, and teaching withall
due remedies therof, wherby not only her fubiects, but
others alfo, euen Prelates
thefelues, & Religious per-
fõs, were profitably affifted.

In the vfe of things for
herfelfe, she was fo truly

K 2   poore

poore, as not the leaſt ſuper-
fluity was admitted by her;
yea want of needfull things,
when at any tyme they hapned, were moſt welcom vn-
to her.

She ſuggeſted alſo no leſ-
ſon, more often to her ſiſters, then that they should
haue alwais theirRedeemers
example before their eyes,
to imitate thoſe Vertues,
which he exerciſed for thé,
and to be carefull to haue a
pure intention in what they
did, only to pleaſe him.

Fortitude and Patience
                              she

she euer prayſed , and commended vnto them, as needfull, and certaine remedies,
victoriouſly to ouercom all
temptations, wherein their
merit more, then in not feeling of them , conſiſted; for
that by this, and not by the
other they should come to
be crowned.

Prayer , she was wont to
tell them, well made, did di
late their ſoules to receaue
plentifull graces , and holy
actions did fill them, when
they were humbly and fer-
uently performed.

CHAP. XX.

How S. Wenefride *was fore-warned of her death, & pre-pared herselfe for the same; And how by acquainting* S. Elerius *and her sisters there-with, she filled their harts full of heauines, and affli-ction.*

S. *VVenefride* as a full Pomegranut of heauenly merits, & ripened to fall on the ground, that she might rise in a new spring, more gloriously afterwards, was

in

in the feruour of her courſe,
& ſpeedy running towards
the goale of religious Perfection , warned by her deare
Lord, that he meant shortly
to call her vnto him.

Which moſt welcome
newes, as of a happineſse
long before , and inſtantly
deſired, rayſed the thoughts
and affections of her ſoule
to a more feruent vnion
with her Creatour, in extaticall prayer for whole dayes
and nights togeather , in
humble acts , and painefull
exerciſes of her Charity to-

wards others; in fasting likewise and other great austeri
ties, euen as those, who to
make a longe iourney in a
short tyme, do redouble &
widen their paces.

And that she might not
leaue her beloued friends
vnwarned of her departure
on the suddaine from them,
she imparted first to *S. Ele-*
rius himselfe, the Call she
had receaued from her Sa-
uiour, and afterwards to her
sisters; whose sorrow thereat was little inferiour to the
excessiue ioy, which her-
selfe,

selfe, by the comfortable
thoughts of going to her
Lord, continually receaued,
and aswell by flowing teares
as dolefull speaches they ex-
pressed the same vnto her.
But she, as with a face then
wholy turned frō the world
towards heauen, intreated
them to conforme their will
to their Creatours pleasure
therein, and not to doubt,
but that she should by her
prayers in heauen, be more
profitable, then by her presence heere on earth she
could be, vnto them.

K 5 For

For that(said she)is not a Country of ignorance, but of knowledge, cleerely reuealed, whereby the Blessed vnderstand their friends necessities heere on earth, and being vnited to the fountayne of Charity it selfe, they will be no lesse powerfull, then ready to procure speedy helps and remedies for them; which I do promise to do for you, my beloued deare Children, after Christ shall take me vnto him.

And whereas (said she)

to other worldly foules vn-
willing to dye, and fearefull
to behold the face of their
high Iudge, whome they are
guilty in their liues, grie-
uoufly to haue offended,
Death commeth as a cruell
iaylor to breake down their
mortery houfes, and to drag
them forcibly vnto him:
So, to holy Soules, he euer
cómeth as a welcom gueft,
and therefore findeth the
dore of their hart open to
receaue him; like vnto men
expecting the returne of
their Lord from his hea-

uenly

uenly wedding, and ready to goe with him, as I am now for that heauenly iourney, with my gracious Lord, throughly (I hope) prepared.

CHAP.

CHAP. XXI.

How S. Wenefride *sickned, &
receaued the last Sacrament;
and what exceeding comfort
she tooke in her death: VVith
a pious Exhortation to her
Religious sisters.*

ALbeit the approach
of death was not ter-
rible, but most delightfull
to *S.VVenefride*, yet was her
sicknes the forerunner, and
naturall cause thereof, by
frequent conuulsions very
painefull vnto her, which
she

she with a glad patience, to goe to her heauenly Spouse, silently sustayned, often and earnestly beseeching him, not to let the infernall Enemy be frightfull vnto her in her last agony.

And finding by her much weaknes, & forces decayed, that her dissolution approached, she called for the Saint her Confessor, to receaue the diuine Sacrament of him, as a safe protection in so dreadfull a passage. And behoulding her sisters kneeling round about her,

and

and grieuing aboue meafure
to loofe her prefence, no
leſſe comfortable then profitable vnto them; Deare
Children (faid she) grieue
not fo, I befeech you, at my
happines thus approaching,
but reioyce rather with me,
that I shall fully now enioy
him in heauen, whome in
earth heere, I haue loued.
Treade alfo, fo neerely as
you can, my footefteps, by
feruing him as I haue done,
& contemning for his fake,
fuch baites, and bafe plea-
fures as the world can af-

foard

foard you. Let your promi-
fed fayth to him be inuiola-
bly obferued , who by his
mercyes and merits is only
able to bring you comfor-
tably to this paffage , and e-
ternally to crowne you. Cõ-
ceaue your bodies , though
youthfull and faire , to be
(as truly they are) but loath-
fome prifons of your foule,
and mortery houfes, apt, if
you take not heed , to pol-
lute, & defile you : and per-
fuade your felues affuredly,
that fo miferable a world as
this is , and full of temptations,

tions, can yield no true happines or pleasures without
daungers vnto you.

To others also that came
to visit her, she ceased not
at times as her voyce would
serue, to giue profitable aduises, & aboue all, that they
should be ready, for that
passage which herselfe then
was entring into; and to
spend their liues in such
sort, as they might receaue
comfort when that moment
should approach, on which
Eternall weale, or woe de-
pendeth.

L CHAP.

CHAP. XXII.

Of S. Wenefrides *happy death and desire to be buried neere* Theonia *, her Mother and Predecessour ; which was by* S. Elerius *accordingly performed: of the miracles likewise wrought at* S. Wenefrides *Sepulcher ; and of* S. Elerius *holy death.*

AS S. VVenefride in the beginning of Nouéber became by her sicknes very much exhausted, so did the ferour of her deuotion,

in

in praying, and speaking of
holy things, seeme conti-
nually increased, by repea-
ting often amongst other
profitable Lessons giuen to
her sisters this one, to wit,
that the cōfort which pure
soules finde in their death,
did aboundantly, recom-
pence all worldly pleasures
and contentments whatsoe-
uer for the seruice of Christ
by them forsaken.

And calling her Father
S. Elerius vnto her, after she
had taken her last leaue of
him, in a most respectfull

L 2   sweet

sweet manner, comforting
herselfe and him also, by a
certaine hope, they shey
should meete againe ere
longe, and liue in heauen e-
ternally togeather; she afterwards humbly besought
him, that her body might
be buried neere vnto *Theo-*
nia her holy Mother, which
the Saint gladly promised .
And soone after, in an act of
feruent prayer, vpon the 3.
day of Nouember she brea-
thed out her pure soule into
her Redeemers hands, rea-
dy to receaue it .

Which

Which being perceaued by *S. Elerius*, and the sisters praying about her, they fall into such new complaints, and sad expressions of their sorrow, that the Saint was enforced, to smother his owne griefe, and to comfort them all he could, by declaring, that she was only gone to Heauen before them, where gloriously, vnited with God, she would be no lesse powerful & ready then when she liued in earth, by her prayers to help them.

Her body nothing chan-

L 3   ged

ged in the louelines thereof by death, was neere vnto
Theonia solemnly afterwards
interred, euen in the ashes,
as it were, of many other
great Saints, buried in that
place before, amōgst whom
Cheb and *Sennan*, the one lying at her head, and the o-
ther by her side, were for
sanctity & miracles in their
dayes famously renowned,
and had Churches therfore
(euen yet remayning in that
Prouince) to their memories
erected; wherein by wonderous signes their glory with

God

God is now frequently te-
ftified.

And albeit thefe two, &
other innumerable Saintes
haue ben interred in that
holy ground; yet was the
fame, for *S. VVenefrides* Sepulcher afterwards efpecially honoured, & graced with
numberles, and notorious
miracles, by her prayers
there obteyned.

S. Elerius alfo, foone after
holily difceafed, & was buried in a Church erected to
his Name and memory, in
which at this very day Al-

L 4   mighty

mighty God, through his merits and prayers worketh miraculous cures vpon perfons either difeafed, or diftreffed.

The End of the firſt Booke.

A N

AN
APPENDIX

*Of the Tranſlatour, concerning
diuers particulars of S. Wenefrids Hiſtory, omitted by
the Author.*

MY Author (Courteous
Reader) more carefull
to write plainely and
truly his Hiſtory, then
to obſerue the conditions of an
exact Hiſtorian, ſpeaketh not of
the tyme wherein *S.Wenefride* liued, as he should haue done; nor
when her body was to *Shrewsbury*

L 5   tranſla

tranſlated; nor whether *S. Elerius*, or other Saints reliques mentio-ned in her life, were with it tranſ-ferred. Wherefore, I will heere adde what I haue read, for your further ſatisfaction.

Firſt therefore, I find in a lear-ned collection which a friend of myne hath made of Britiſh and Engliſh Antiquities, either who-ly omitted, or obſcurely expreſ-ſed by other writers; that *S. Wene-fride* liued about the yeare of Chriſt 660. And wheras *S. Bede* flouriſhing alſo at that tyme hath made no mention of her at all in his History, amongſt the other Saints of our Countrey; it might well happen, becauſe the conti-nuall iarrs, and bloudy quarrels between the *Britans* and *Saxons*,

did

did so hinder all commerce betweene thefe two Nations, as
that it feemes the Acts of one
Church became almoft wholy
vnknowne vnto the other, efpecially in Yorkefhyre, where *S.
Bede* moft commonly liued, far di-
ftant from any part of Wales : fo
as his filence of her, and of *S. Elerius* (in the Roman martyrologe
acknowledged) as of many other
Britifh Saintes glorioufly flouri-
fhing in thofe dayes, and before
infinuated alfo by my Author,
difproueth nothing that is by
him, or any other learned Anti
quary affirmed.

Her body was in the yeare of
our Lord 1138. tranflated to
Shrewsbury, togeather with the reli
ques of many other Saintes neere

vnto

vnto hers formerly interred. And
for proofe hereof, besides the testimonies of Authors, about 36
yeares since, a Protestant Gentleman willing to pleasure a learned friend of mine, whome he
knew to be Catholique, presented
him with an arme, as he said, of
S.Wenefride, saued by some body
when her Shrine was defaced.
The which he finding not decently kept, but put into a very old
leather bag full of Cobwebs (as
himselfe hath tould me)taking it
out, more decently to adorne it,
found in a paper fixed thereon,
somewhat written in an old hād,
so as with much difficulty he read
at last these words, *Sancti Elerij*;
whereby he vnderstood, that it
was not the arme of *S.Wenefride*,

but

but of *S. Elerius*, tranflated doubt-
leffe with her, or foone after , to
Shrewsbury .

Hauing likewife conferred with
diuers learned men of *Wales*, neither fuperftitious, nor ouercredu-
lous to belieue Fables, or vncer-
tainties , they haue tould me of fo
many places in fundry parts of
Wales, northwards efpecially , famous heeretofore, as pilgrimages
to Saintes bodies there interred,
that I conceaue the old *Brittifh*
Monkes and Hermits, in number
and religious fanctity of life, not
to haue ben inferiour to thofe primitiue Monkes of *Egypt*, *Paleftine*,
Syria, and other places, by *S. Atha-
nafius*, *S. Hierome*, & other ancient
Fathers famoufly renowned ; albeit as liuing in more remote &

ruder

ruder parts of the world then the
others did , the histories of their
holy liues haue not been by learned mens pens equally diuulged.

In so much , as *M.Camden*, no
fauourable reporter of such Catholique Acts and Monuments,
rarely now extant , speaking of
the old british Monkes of *Glasten-
bury* Monastery from the first A-
postolicall tymes of that Church,
hath these wordes , in his *Britan-
nia : Primis his temporibus viri san-
ctissimi &c* . In these first tymes
(to wit of the British Church before the *Saxons* inuasion of England , more then 1100. yeares
since) many most holy men night
and day attending to the seruice
of God, liued in this place, maintayned by the Kings liberality

and

and trayning vp youth in piety &
liberal sciences, imbraced a solitary life, that so with greater quiet
& repose they might attend to the
studies of Diuinity, and exercise
themselues in all seuerity, to beare
the Christ of Christ &c. Of which
sort of Monkes so by him descri-
bed, were very many Religious
men, dispersed in like manner
though all parts of that Church,
liuing either in holy Communi-
ties as Monkes, or els alone as
Hermites in solitary places; of
which number were *S. Beuno*, *S.*
Saturnus, *S. Deifer*, *S. Elerius*, *S.*
Cheb, and *S. Sennan* mentioned in
this life of *S. VVenefrid.*

And, as Godly men, so Holy
Virgins also, did liue in houses
religiously togeather, like vnto

those

thole mentioned by *S. Hicrome*, who liued at *Bethleem*, vnder *S. Paula*, and *Eustochium* her Daughter : & such was the house wherin *S. Wenefride* liued, first at *Finhon* the place of her martyrdome, and afterwards at *Guitherin* (called in Latin *Witheriacum* by my Author) where she dyed happily, and was honoured 600. yeares together for a Saint, vntill her sollemne translation, as is aforesaid, to *Shrewsbury*; where also she hath byn by God glorified with many miracles euen vntill our dayes, as she had byn before both at *Finhon*, and *Guitherin*, the places aboue mentioned.

THE

THE SECOND BOOKE,
conteyning the miracles wrought
at *S. Wenefrides Well*; as alſo
vpon her Tranſlation
to *Shrewsbury*.

CHAP. I.

*Of the great-concourſe of people
to her* Well, *graced by miracles, no leſſe then before,
after her departure from
that place.*

ALmighty God ceaſed
not by wonderfull

M   mira-

miracles to grace the holy
place of *S. VVenefrids* martyrdome, after he had in-
spired her (as hath ben said)
before her death wholy to
abandone it, to the end deuout people, perchance, in
other parts of the Country
might come to know the e-
minent sanctity of her life,
and herselfe perfect the graces of her soule, by liuing
humbly, and obediently a-
mongst strangers, as she did
for many yeares, vntill by
her singular merits & exemplar life, she was ordeyned

againſt

against her will, to be a holy
Miftreffe and gratefull Go-
uerneffe of many Virgins.

We may alfo conceaue,
that this humble Virgin,
(who was wont to blush,
yea and shed teares, when
she heard herfelfe prayfed)
defired, & obteyned of her
heauenly Spoufe, to goe out
of the way, as it were, and
abfent herfelfe from that
place, where she could not
choofe but be feene, and honoured by multitudes of
people, daily vifitting her
VVell, as the miraculous

Trophy of her martyrdome there sufteyned; wondring firft, to fee fuch a fource of pure water breaking out of the ground vpon which her head firft fell; next, to behould the ftones therein, as with drops of her bloud ftrangly ftayned, or died rather; and laftly to fmell the greene moffe growing about the *VVell*, with a mufky fweet odour more then naturally perfumed.

It was (I fay) a pleafure no doubt, and much by the holy Virgin defired, to liue out of the noise of her owne prayses there daily resounded; especially when to the wonders of the place it selfe, other miraculous Cures began to be wrought vpon leaprous, blind, and all kind of diseased persons, either by drinking of the water, or bathing themselues in it: of which some few, in the Chapters following shalbe by me declared.

CHAP.

CHAP. II.

Of a blind maid restored to her sight, by washing her head in S. Wenefrids Well, and praying in her Chappell.

A POORE Carpenter dwelling not far from S. Wenefrides Well, had a Daughter borne blind, who hauing hard of the wonderfull cures wrought there, by the intercession and merits of that holy Virgin, ceased not to importune her Father daily, that she might

be

be ledd to that miraculous
VVell; and hauing finally
obteyned the fame, she firft
bathed her head in the water thereof, and then be-
ing conducted to the Chappell neere vnto it , she spent
the whole night deuoutely
in prayer , that God would
be pleased through the merits and interceffion of the
Saint , there martyred for
his fake, to beftow vpon her
corporall fight , the better
to ferue him afterwards : &
falling into a flumber , towards the morning in a cor-

ner of the Chappell, she was no sooner awaked, but she found herselfe to see perfectly; which being perceaued by her Father, he ceased not, togeather with his Daughter, ioyfully to proclayme that miraculous fauour by *S. VVenefrids* powerfull prayers, euidently obteyned.

The fame of this miracle generally diuulged, bred a fresh deuotion in others, to repayre in like manner to that place, for obteyning help, and comfort in their

cor-

corporall and spirituall distresses ; and they were not
frustrated of their hopes,
faythfully, and deuoutely
so conceaued : whereby the
former great Fame of the
place, became more vniuersally and glorioufly diuulged, to the honour of him,
by whose omnipotency and
gracious goodnes these miraculous cures were multi-
plied , delightfully glorified in the honours done to
his Saintes , and in their
glories eternally exalted.

M 5 CHAP.

CHAP. III.

*How a Theefe was punished
for purſuing one that fled
into S. Wenefrids Church:
And how the ſame man, humbled for his fault, was mira-
culouſly ſaued from death.*

IT happened that a meſ-
ſenger ſent by a Chiefe
Lord of that Country, to
warne his Neighbours of
ſome danger approaching
frō the *Saxons* their Borde-
rers, and alwayes common-
ly in enmity with them,

was

was way-layd by Theeues,
and pursued towards *S.VVe-*
nefrids Church , whither as
to a safe Sanctuary he fled ,
and haftily tying his horse
at the Church dore , ranne
himselfe vp to the Aultar,
where the Theeues , not
daring to pursue him fur-
ther , left him , but tooke
away his horse .

The meffenger after their
departure , returning to-
wards the dore , and fin-
ding his horse gone , entred
againe very dolefully into
the Church , and proftrate

before

before the Aultar, vttered
his cõplaintes to the Saint
of the iniury, and losse ther-
by sustained, beseeching her
to punish, as they deserued
the wrongfull Authors of
that and other mischiefes,
to the great harme of ho
nest people sinfully com-
mitted, and by some exem-
plar reuenge taken vpon
them, to warne, and deterre
others, from violating in
like manner, the safety of
her Chappel, and reuerence
due vnto it; and so departed
onwards in his iourney, not

fru-

frustrate afterward of what
he had prayed for.

For Almighty God , in
honour of *S. VVenefrid* and
her Chappell, forthwith af-
flicted the Theefe that had
vnloofed, and taken away
the horfe , with fuch a raging extremity of payne,
throughout his whole body,
that he often defired to be
freed by death from fo in-
tollerable a torment, daily
increafing on him, till the
humours which caufed the
fame, fel into his right arme,
making it firft to fwell, and

after-

afterwards to rot in a most horrible, and loathesome manner, vntill at length humbled by affliction, and hopeles of all ease otherwise he came in a very penitent manner, to the Saints chappell, confessing his fault, & demaunding her pardon, with many teares, for so great a wrong and insolency committed there by him.

Vpon this his humiliation he became eased by degrees, and by little and little cured of his paineful vlcer, praysing God, and the holy

Martyr

Martyr for their mercyes
towards him, & remayning
euer afterwards whilst he
liued , a dreadfull exam-
ple, to warne others , from
violating , as he had done,
the sanctity of that place,
or wronging *S. VVenefrids*
clients running for succour
in their distresses vnto her.

The Fame also of this
miracle diuulged abroad,
increased much the peoples
opinion of the place, and
their deuotion towards the
Saint ; who had shewed herselfe so powerfull a Patronesse

neffe of her Chappell, and Defendreffe of fuch, as for their fafety, and prote- ction from iniuries, repay- red vnto it.

CHAP.

CHAP. IV.

How certaine Theeues who had
stolne a Cow neere to S.We-
nefrids Chappell, and driuen
her through Rocky wayes,
were notwithstanding tra-
ced by her footesteps in the
hard stones miraculously im-
printed, and so enforced to
leaue her to the Owners pur-
suing them.

ANother Miracle, no lesse wonderfull then the former hapned in this manner. Certaine Theeues

hauing ſtolne a Cow, out
of a paſture neere to *S. VVe-*
nefrids Chappell, & driuen
her through Rocky high
wayes, that they might not
by her footing be traced, it
fell out far otherwiſe: for the
Cow trod not one ſteppe,
but as if ſhe had gone in
durty deepe wayes, wherby
her footing, and the theues
alſo themſelues, ſo plainely
appeared, that the owner &
his Neighbours, the next
morning miſſing the beaſt,
did very eaſily ſee which
way ſhe was driuen.

Where-

Whereupon they following the tracke with all speed, came so neere to ouertake the Theeues, that they were constreyned in great feare to fly away, and leaue the Cow behind them to their pursuers. VVho at better leasure afterwardes considering how the Cowes feet had miraculously made prints in the hard stones as she was driuen away, but not as she returned, perceaued it to be an euident miracle, and for such, to the honour of *S. VVenefride*, by

N , whose

whose prayers it hapned,
they diuulged the same,
through out the **whole**
Countrey;&the infinite nūbers of people flocking thither to see the said printes in
the stones so straūgly made
by the Cowes feet,increased
the fame thereof.

Now the theeues them-
selues , fearing for their
theft committed so neere
vnto the Saintes Chap-
pell, to be punished by her,
as the other had bene be-
fore, for stealing the horse
mentioned in the former

Chapter

Chapter , came of théselues
before the Virgin Martyrs
Aultar, and confessed penitently their fault in the presence of many people, with
promise to commit the like
no more, in honour of the
Blessed Saint, who had in so
strang a manner, discouered
in hard stones, and flints,
the tracke of their owne,
and of the Cowes footings.
Which fact of theirs being
thus discouered, & volun-
tarily confessed, proued a
generall warning to many
other bad men of that ta-

king-trade, to abſtayne like-wiſe from theft, eſpecially out of any place, neere to the Saintes Chappels.

CHAP.

CHAP. V.

Of daily Cures done vpon ficke children throwne into the ftreame of S. VVenefrids VVell; and of others alfo cured miraculoufly of agues, & hoat feauers, by drinking of the fame water .

IN procefse of tyme, this facred Fountayne, the Trophy, and triumphant figne of *S. VVenefrids* Martyrdome, became fo famoufly renowned, for miraculous cures done by the wa-

N 4   ters

ters thereof, that Mothers were vſually wont to throw their young children ſicke of any diſeaſe, into the ſtreame running from the ſame, who became preſently cured, by the touch of thoſe waters.

Such alſo as had Agues, or hoat burning Feauers in any part of the Country, were wont for a certaine and preſent remedie therof, either to drincke a draught of that pure fountaine-water, or if they had it not at hand, to put in ſome one of

the

the blouddy ftones, taken
out. of the VVell , into a
draught of any other water,
and became thereby pre-
fently cured . In like máner
fuch as had any fwelling or
foare about them, were accu-
ftomed to bath the part affected, with the faid water,
and found prefent remedy
thereby.

The firft vfe of which
remedies , for all forts of
fores and difeafes, is faid to
haue ben taught by the holy Virgin-Martyr herfelfe,
who vifibly after her death

appearing to many who in dangerous sicknesse deuoutely called vpon her, willed them to apply the water & stones of her well in máner aforesaid, for their perfect, and speedy recouery : Almighty God cótinuing still, to grace this glorious Monument of his deare spouses death, by affoarding helpe thereby to such, as either deuoutely repaire vnto it, or faithfully seeke remedies fró it; according to *S. Beuno* his holy prediction, whé before his departure fró those

parts

parts he fate vpon a ftone
with *S. VVenefride* herfelfe ,
neere to the Wels fide, and
foretould the miraculous
cures which should throgh
her merits and prayers be at
the fame, afterwards per-
formed.

CHAP.

CHAP. VI.

How diuers thefts from places neere vnto the Well, *were by* S. Wenefride *miraculously punished ; and how the Authors became warned and penitent for the same.*

THE streames of wa-
ter breaketh out of
Saint VVenefrides VVell, in
such abundance togeather,
as within one furlongs space
it driueth a mill, neuer standing still for want of water
euen in the greatest drought

of

of summer, nor is euer hindred from grinding, by any freezing of the streame, by which it is driuen in winter.

This Mill, by certaine theeues, was vpon a tyme robbed in the night, and the Irons thereof were carried away to be put into another mill built not far frō thence by those that stole them: but through the merits of *S. VVenefride* a strange euent hapned heer about for the Mill into which these Irons were put, could neuer be

made

made to turne, or grind any
thing therewith : fo as the
ftealers thereof mooued at
length by the miracle more
thé once experiéced, broght
them back againe, and con-
feffed their fault penitently
in the Saintes Chappell;
warning others thereby not
to commit the like theft in
placesneere vnto it for feare
of beeing, by her prayers,
punished for it.

By this Miracle fo diuul-
ged, many peopie alfo were
moued the more to glorify
God, in thofe wonderous

things which he did, to te-
stifie, the great merits of
this holy Virgin *S. VVene-*
fride, ioyfully relating to
one another, how *S. Beuno's*
prediction of the innume-
rable Cures which should
be done by those miracu-
lous waters, and by the Virgins owne prayers, began to
be now fulfilled, when as
humbly prostrate on her
knees before her departure
frō that place, she besought
her heauenly spouse, corpo-
rally to blesse, and spiritually to sanctifie those who in

ho-

honour of him, and his graces in herselfe, should in future tymes visit that Fountayne.

And as wonderfull, yea almost daily, miracles graced this place thus blessed by her; so was her Sepulcher after her death, for the like Cures wrought thereat, equally illustrious & renowned by the multitudes of blind, deafe, lazar, & diseased people, who by kissing and touching the earth about it, were miraculously cured.

CHAP.

CHAP. VII.

Of the first occasion of Transla-
ting S. Wenefrids *reliques*
to the Monastery of Benedi-
cta Monkes in Shrewsbury,
happened vpon a vision to a
holy Monke in Chester, *of*
the same Order.

T He miraculous cures
daily wrought at *S.*
VVenefrids VVell, and at the
place of her Sepulcher also,
continued vntill the raigne
King *VVilliam the Conqueror,*
at what time a chiefe Earle

O   of

of his Court, called *Roger*, through his great piety and zeale to mantayne Gods seruants, built in *Shrewsbury* a sumptuous faire Monastery, and endowed the same with sufficient reuenewes, to his owne great prayse, and the benefit of that Citty: which Monastery being ended, & Religious men with their Superiour placed therin, they began, piously to complayne that they wāted reliques in their Church, whereas that Country of *VVales* in innumerable pla-

ces

ces was stored aboundantly
with them, by reason of so
many great Saintes, men &
women, who formerly had
flourished in great sanctity
of life, and miraculous te-
stifications therof, throughout that whole Kingdome.

Whereupon to haue their
Church hallowed, & their
new Monastery guarded
with such sacred pledges,
munificetly placed, & duly
honoured by thē, they begā
to inquire after some spe-
ciall Saint, whose Reliques
might happily be gotten for

that purpose by them; during which deliberation of theirs, a Monke of this their Monastery, fell very sicke, in body, and so distracted in mind withall, that not only his Brethren there, but in *Chester* and other places also, hearing of his pittifull case, ceased not to pray most hartily for him.

And as in *Chester-Abbey*, the Subprior of that Monastery, a godly man, called *Radulphus*, had one day ended his prayer for that end,

he

he fell into an vnusuall kind
of sleepe, to whome a wo-
man, the meane while, in a
very glorious habit appeared, and said : If you desire
the sicke Monks health, let
some one of you goe, & say
a Masse in the Chappell,
neere *S. VVenefrids VVell* for
him, and he shall presently
recouer; & so she vanished.

The Moncke heerewith
awaked, durst not for some
tyme impart this vision vnto any, as fearing little credit would be giuen vnto
it, vntill at length, the

ficknes and great diftemper
of his deare Brother lamentably ftill increafing, charitably moued him to fpeake
thereof vnto his brethren,
who prefently belieued the
fame, and that it was *S. VVe-*
nefride herfelfe who had appeared vnto him. Wherfore
fending forthwith two of
their Company to the for-
faid Chappell, to fay Maffe
accordingly, the ficke Mōke
at that very inftant, being
then in *Shrewsbury*, recoue-
red his health.

Who foone after this his

mira-

miraculous recouery, came
himselfe in person, vnto the
said Chappell and Well, as
he greatly desired, to giue
God thankes for the same;
and after hauing bathed
himselfe in the water, and
also druncke therof, he ioyfully returned home to
Shrewsbury perfectly cured:
neuer ceasing afterwards to
be thankefull to God, and
the Blessed Martyr, for that
gracions fauour, by her
prayers chiefly obteyned.

And not only he, but the
rest of his Brethren like-

wise began to bè singularly deuoted vnto her, and laboured by all meanes possible to get some particle of her Virginall sacred Body vnto them.

CHAP.

CHAP. VIII.

Of the earnest desire which the Abbot & Monkes of Shrewsbury *had to get the body of* S. VVenefride *vnto them: And how finally after many yeares, & very great difficulties, they obteyned the same.*

THe Abbot & Monks of *Shrewsbury,* for many yeares persisting in their holy desires, of getting *S.* VVenefrides body, obteyned at length in the peacefull reigne of King *Henry* the firſt a Grant therof, but by reaſon of wars, and many tumults happening in that Countrey after this Kings death, it was not effected vntill the ſecōd yeare of King *Stephens* reigne, when as the holy Abbot *Herbert* in a conſultation of his Monkes, ordeyned *Robert* his Prior, togeather with one *Richard*, a chiefe Monke of the ſame Monaſtery, to go into *VVales* about it.

Before whoſe going, the ſaid *Robert*, more ſolicitous

then

then others in the businesse,
directed diuers letters vnto
friends in *VVales*, best likely
therein to assist him, who
promised gladly their help,
& wished him to hasten his
coming amōgst thē. Wher-
fore beginning his iourney
he first visitted the Bishop
of *Bangor*, in his way, and
was by him directed to a
Principall Lord who ruled
in that Country, & by him
him very courteously re-
ceaued.

As soone as the Noble
Man, had vnderstocd the

cause

cause of his cōming : Reue-
red Father (said he) I doubt
not, but that God, and the
Blessed Martyr hath sent
you to translate her holy
body, to your Monastery,
where it will be much more
honoured then heere in this
Countrey it is. VVherfore I
will not only yield you my
consent therennto, but will
send also my seruants therein to assist you. And sinfull
man, as I am, did not my
present, and very important
businesses, hinder me, I
would presume to goe with

you

you in perſon, and with my
vnworthy handes, deliuer
thoſe ſacred Reliques, and
Pledge of Sanctity, vnto
you.

VVith which gracious
anſwere they departed to-
wards the Saints Sepulcher,
being ſeauen in number, to
wit, the two Priours of
Shrewsbury & *Cheſter*, *Richard*
the Monke, with a godly
Prieſt borne in that Country, and three attendants;
who going onwards in their
iourney, not far from *Gui-*
therine they met with a man
that

that tould them, how the Inhabitants therabout, hauing heard of their comminge, were exceedingly troubled thereat, and abſolutely reſolued to hinder them in their pretence, and not to ſuffer the chiefe Saint, & Patroneſſe of their Countrey, by ſtrangers to be carried away from them. And (ſaid he) from this their reſolution generally taken, no fauour or power of any man liuing, will be able to draw them.

Theſe words being plai

nely and sincerely vttered,
very much troubled Prior
Robert and his companions
all that night; but yet praying all togeather, and humbly crauing Gods direction
& assistáce in their intéded
busines, they neuerthelesse
aduentured , to prosecute
their iourney , & comming
the next day neere to the
place , Prior *Robert* thought
good to remaine himselfe
in a Farmers house , pri-
uatly lodged that night, and
to send the *Prior* of *Chester*
and the other Priest to *Gui-*

therine

therine before him , as men well borne, and knowne in that Country .

After they were gone , Prior *Robert* , rising as his custome was by night to say his mattins, was certified by one of his company, a good deuout man, that a glorious Virgin had appeared that night to him , bidding him goe to his Prior, & tell him from her, that he should be of good comfort, becaufe he should ioyfully and profperoufly , effect the bufines which he came for, by the

help

help of her, whose honour he hath so particularly sought; and hauing accepted of his holy intention, will ioyne also with him, in the performance therof.

CHAP.

CHAP. IX.

How Prior Robert *himselfe had a vision, whereby he vnderstood, that he should obteyne the body of* S. Wenefride *, and carry it vnto* Shrewsbury *with him.*

THe Prior much comforted with the relation of the vision which his seruant, as before had made vnto him, began to slumber after his Mattins ended, & in his sleepe seemed to see a holy Abbot of his owne

Mona-

Monastery, called *Godfrey*, who some yeares before in a good old age, and great sanctity of life was happily disceased, vttering these words comfortably vnto him. Brother *Robert*, feare not of fayling in your intent, but be of good cheere, for we shal ouercome such as shall oppose vs therein, by Gods helpe, and obteyne what hath ben by vs, for many yeares togeather so earnestly desired.

Which said, he vanished presently away, leauing the

Prior full of good hope, to obteyne that, which his speach imported; so as in the morning, he comfortably declared to those who were with him the vision he had also receaued, and willed them, therefore to prepare presently for their iourney. But before they were ready, a messenger came from the other Prior purposely sent, to hasten them forwards & to certifie them withall, that Almighty God, and the Saint herselfe had disposed all things, so prosperously,

for

for them, that they should
not returne without obteyning what they desired.

This ioyfull message re-
ceaued, they went on, and
making what speede they
could, they came early in
the morning to the Church
where *S.* VVenefrides body
was certainely interred, and
hauing for a while at her
shrine deuoutely prayed,
the chiefe Priest of the Parish came in, and courteously saluted them, as they did
him likewise in a very humble manner, earnestly in-

trea-

treating him withall, to be their charitable helper, in carrying away the Saintes body with them, to a place where it should be more magnificently interred then there it was, and daily honoured, by multitudes of people, defirous to haue fo facred a **Treafure** repofed amongft them.

CHAP.

CHAP. X.

How the Parish Priest cour-
teously condeſcended to their
deſire, as hauing byn before
hand diuinely prepared, to
deliuer the body of S. Wene-
fride ᴠnto them.

THe good Prieſt pa-
tiently hard their re-
queſt, and courteouſly tould
them, that he for his part,
would eaſily graunt what
they deſired of him, as hauing had for ſometyme be-
fore, the will of God, and of

the sacred Virgin herselfe,
intimated vnto him, as now
(said he) I shall briefly tell
you.

On Easter Eue last, i
watching all night in this
place, had a vision which
exceedingly affrighted me,
for a beautifull young man
appeared vnto me, scarsely
then a sleepe, and fully wa-
kening me, bad me rise. To
whome I answered, that it
was not as yet tyme to be-
gin mattins, and so he left
me. But returning the se-
cond time when I was much

more

more then before soundly a-
sleepe, he bad me rise as he
had done before. Whereu-
pon beeing very heauy, I
tould him, that I would rise
in due tyme, and couering
my head with my cloake,
returned to sleepe agayne.

But he, returning the
third tyme vnto me, pulled
away my cloake with great
force, willing me to follow
him quickly, as I did, being
very much affrighted: and
comming to the Virgins
Shrine, he pointed with his
fingar towards it, and said:

Note this place well, & my
words alfo, whereby I do
command thee, that if fome
moneths hence any perfons
come to opé this Sepulcher,
& to carry away fhe Saintes
body with them, hinder
them not in their holy de-
figne, but affift them in all
thou maift, leaft by dooing
contrary to what I heere diuinely foretell thee, fome
painefull & vnremediable
ficknes, to punifh thy difo-
bedience, do happen vnto
thee. And hauing vtte-
red thefe words, this Angel,

as

as I thinke he was, vanished away. So as I wil not faile for my part, to help you in your purpoſe, by perſuading others alſo, who are owners of this village, to yield willingly the Saints body: and for this purpoſe I haue ordeined them to come themſelues hither vnto you.

CHAP.

CHAP. XI.

*The Priours speach vnto the
people assēbled in the Church,
about obteyning their leaue
to carry away S. Wene-
frids Body; and how their
consent was finally obteyned.*

THe Priour seeing the
people in great num-
bers assembled, by an Inter-
preter tould them, that he
and his Companions were
come, diuinely warranted,
to procure of them S. *VVenefrids* body, that in their

Citty

Citty, and Monastery much deuoted vnto her, it might more thē it could be there, honoured and respected; & the Blessed Virgin Martyr herselfe (said he) as your Pastour heere partly knoweth) hath by many visions manifested her willingnes hereunto, and will not be pleased with such as shall dare heerein to resist her. To which speach of his, they gently harkened, and became inclined thereby to graunt what he requested: one only amongst them op-

posed

posed himselfe, and clamo-
rously tould them in pre-
sence of the rest, that they
should neuer be depriued,
by his will, of so sacred a
Treasure, as was the body
of that Saint, who had liued
holily, and dyed happily in
that place, leauing her reliques to be honoured by
them, no lesse then they
had ben by their Ancestors
before them, Allmighty
God hauing from tyme to
tyme, by miracles, appro-
ued the pious deuotion of
people towards them.

                        This

This paſſionate boldnes
of the man much troubled
the Prior, ſo as to ſtop his
mouth, and gayne his con-
ſent, he cauſed one of his
cōpany to giue him money
very largely, by which he
was ſo altered, as that others
not knowing the reaſon of
his change (carefully from
them concealed) wondered
thereat; and imputing the
ſame to ſome miraculous
operation wrought by God
and the Saint, began to
yield their owne conſents
ſomewhat more willingly,

then

then before, and finally after many consultations passed among themselues, at last they all fully agreed,& consented that the Saintes body should be presently taken vp, and deliuered decently vnto them.

For which resolution the Prior and his companions very hartily & courteously gaue them thankes,& without any delay desired to enter the holy Ile , wherin the Saintes Shrine had ben for many ages deuoutely visitted by holy Pilgrims , and

many

many wonderfull cures v-
pon diseased pesons fre-
quently performed.

Neither did they find
her body there alone, but
many holy bodies both of
men and women also were
found lying by it; hauing
without the place of their
buriall, a woodden lardge
porch, wherein the people
vsed to kneele and pray;
esteemed also sacred of it
selfe for this continuall miracle, that if any beast came
to feed of the grasse neere
vnto it, it presently dyed; &

Q men

men themſelues exemplarly
punished, if at any tyme
they committed any irre-
uerence, or vnſeemly thing
therein.

CHAP.

CHAP. XII.

How a certaine man had beene exemplarly punished, two yeares before the Priours comming to Guitherine, for offering to cut downe a branch of an old Oake which grew neere the Martyrs Shrine, seruing for a shade to the Pilgrimes resorting thither; and how he was by S. Wenefride miraculously released.

AMONGST frequent & very euident mi-

racles wrought at *Guitherin*
Church, by *S. VVenefride*,
and other Saintes there interred, this one as freshly
happened, was vnto the
Prior and his companions
thus certainely recounted.

A certaine labouring
man two yeares before, pre-
sumed, for some vse, to cut
downe a bough of an old
Oake, growing neere the
Church dore in holy groūd
yielding also a conuenient
shade, and shelter to such
deuout pilgrimes as could
not sometimes enter into

the

the Church for the Con-
courſe of people, but were
forced to ſtay without, and
pray vnder it : Who had
no ſooner ſtrooke his Hatchet into the bough, but
it became therein immo-
ueabl y fixed, and his whole
hand and arme did like-
wiſe cleaue ſo faſt vnto the
handle of the hatchet, that
they ſeemed to haue grown
vnto it, & by no force were
able to be remoued.

The poore man finding
himſelfe in this diſtreſſe,
cried out for help, which his

Q 3   neigh-

neighbours hearing , they came running to the place, but finding him in that most pittifull plight, stood amazed at the miracle, as not able any way to help him. Wherfore by their ad-uise he began to repent him of his fault, and humbly besought, amõgst the other Saints , *S. VVenefrid* to help him. The rest also ioyning in like prayer with him, after they had cryed aloud and all togeather, *Holy VVe-nefride take pitty on him* , his hand was presently loosed

from

from the hatchet, and his
arme to all freedome restored.

Which euident miracle
seene by the people, they re-
newed their wonted vene-
ration to the Saint. They
shewed also vnto Priour
Robert and his companions,
the Cut which the man had
made in the branch of the
tree, remayning still for a
testimony thereof: so as
with very good reason, they
all much reuerenced that
holy place, by innumerable
miracles so diuinely graced.

Q 4 　　CHAP.

CHAP. XIII.

How Priour Robert *, the Author of this historie, did himselfe take ʋp the holy body of* S. VVenefride, *and carry it towards* Shrewsbury; *How also in the way, he wrought a miracle by some of the earth, found in the Holy head of that Blessed Martyr.*

PRior *Robert* hauing had a generall leaue from the Pastour of the Church and his parishioners to take

vp

vp the Saintes body, went
downe without a guide in-
to her Tõbe or Sepulcher,
and by an interiour light,
communicated then diui
nely vnto him, knowing
where it lay, cauſed the
Tombeſtone to be remo-
ued, and labourers to digge
towards the body; which
when they had found, the
Prior cauſing them to goe
forth out of the Vault, he
only with ſome Prieſts and
Religious perſons, ſtayed
behind, ſinging pſalmes of
ioy deuoutely togeather, &

Q 5   ta-

taking vp the holy bones, togeather with the next earth that lay about them, he caufed them to be put into a fine linnen Cloth, which he had brought for that purpofe, & fo deuoutly wrapped them togeather.

With which holy Burden, after he had hartily thanked the Paftour of the Church, & the reft of thofe Inhabitants, for fo facred a Treafure beftowed vpon him, he with his Company rode that night backwards in their iourney, and being

lodged

lodged by an honest Far-
mer in their way, they heard
a man in some remote part
of the house pittifully to
groane, and often cry out
through the painefullnes
of his sicknes. Wherefore
the good Priour enquiring
where was, went to visit
him, & commiserating his
case, tooke a little water
and blessed it, putting ther-
into a little of the earth
which he found in *S. VVenefrids* head, & caused the
party to drinke it; which
was no sooner passed downe

into

into the ficke mans fto-
mack, but he fell foundly a-
fleepe, and when he awa-
ked, found himfelfe of his
daungerous and painefull
infirmity perfectiy reco-
uered.

By which moft euident
Miracle, the credit of thofe
facred reliques, to the great
ioy of the Priour himfelfe
and his companions, was
diuinely confirmed, and
the deuotion of all prefent
towards them increafed.
Others alfo there prefent
did learne from thence,

what

what due veneration & re-
uerence was to be yielded
afterwards vnto them.

CHAP.

CHAP. XIV.

How Priour Robert *, after
seauen dayes iourney , arri-
uing with the sacred Reliques at* Shrewsbury *, was
by his Abbot commanded to
place them in* S. Giles *his
Church neere the gate of that
Citty , vntill all was ready
for their sollemne receauing
into the Monastery :* VVith
*a notable miracle which hap-
pened in that place.*

PRior *Robert* & his company in seauen dayes

ended

ended their iourney backe
againe with the facred treafure to *Shrewsbury* ; and hauing before giuen notice
to the Abbot of their ap-
proach, they were willed by
him to ftay, and repofe the
fame decently in *S. Giles* his
Church neere the gate of
the Citty, that the Lord Bishop and his Clergy , with
the reft of the people might
be warned therof, and in fol-
léne proceffion bring them
to the Monaftery.

And for the greater honor
of them in the meane time,

the

the Monks were appointed
night and day, in their tur-
nes , to watch and pray deuoutely before them , ac-
companied alwayes in their
prayers with multitudes of
the people , hartily delighted at such vnusuall Treasures bought vnto them.
Neither did the Saint faile
by many miraculous cures
of sick persons , to requite
this her deuout entertayn-
ment ; one amongst the rest
was especially noted, and so
great a one indeed , as it de-
serueth heere to be particu-

larly

larly recounted, wrought vpon a younge man, who had layne long miserably diseased, and so in his limbs contracted, that he could not stand, or lift vp his head from his knees, towardes heauen.

This man moued with the fame of these Reliques and miraculous cures, frequently wrought by them at *S. Giles* Church, desired to be carried thither, and set before the Aultar whereon the Sacred Reliques were placed. Where after he had

R   prayed

prayed all the night that
God through the merits &
prayers of great *S. VVenefrid*,
would be pleaſed to cure
him , he fell towardes the
morning into a ſlumber, and
before the Prieſt came to
ſay the firſt maſſe, he was to
the wonder of all preſent,
& of the whole Citty like-
wiſe , perfectly cured, and
made whole; ſo as after he
had ſoūded forth thankeful
prayſes to God & the holy
Martyr, he returned with-
out help of others ioyfully
homewards on his feet.

CHAP.

CHAP. XV.

VVith what solemnity & pompe
S. Wenefrides *body was*
brought ᴠnto *the Abbey-*
Church *of* Shrewsbury :
And of a ſtrange Miracle
which happened thereat .

THE former miracle
increaſed much the
fame of theſe holy Reli-
ques brought into the Citty , and the opinion alſo
of *S.VVenefrids* ſanctity , ſo
that the cōcourſe of people
was very great, daily hono-

ring the holy Virgin in
them. Priour *Robert* in the
meane tyme hauing by or-
der of his Abbot, treated
with the Bishop about the
solemnity of bringing her
body frō *S.Giles* his Church
to the Monastery ; it was a-
greed betweene them, that
the people of the Citty and
Country likewise should be
warned of the certaine day
whē this solénity should be
kept, and the Bishops blef-
sing & indulgences for such
a feast promulgated, to all
that should be present in

the

the procession.

Whereupon, the throng of people kneeling on ech side of the ſtreetes & shedding teares of ioy for ſuch a bleſſing, brought amongſt them, was ſo great, that it was a wōder to ſee how gratefull their deuotion was to God, and to the Saint thus honored by them. At which tyme alſo hapned an euident miracle in the ſight of all, worthy heere to be related.

The morning wherein this ſolemne proceſſion was

to be made , began to be all
ouercaſt with darke clouds ,
threatning preſent rayne ,
which had it fallen , would
haue cauſed no doubt great
nūbers to haue withdrawne
themſelues , for feare of
ſpoyling their beſt and co-
ſtly apparell , and ſo haue
leſſened the ſolénity intended . But the Godly , and
Religious Monkes , togea-
ther with the whole Clergy
moſt earneſtly beſought the
Diſpoſer of all ſeaſons and
tymes, to graunt them dry
weather for the comfort of

good

good people, and honour of
his Saint, vntill the proceffion at leaft were ended.

And their prayers to this
effect, became fo effectuall
with his diuine Maiefty,
that although abundant of
raine fell in all other places
of the Citty, and fields a-
bout it; yet no one droppe
thereof fell in the ftreetes
where the body paffed: fo as
all the people prefent, were
greatly amazed to behould
mayne showers, as it were,
of rayne, a'ready powred
out of the cloudes, to hange

R 4   mira-

miraculoufly in the ayre,
ouer their heads, and yet be
kept from falling downe
vpon them, till the folemni-
ty was ended : and therfore
they redoubled their praifes
to God, and to the Saint, as
Authors of this great mi-
racle wrought euidently before their face.

The Proceffion ended
and the Bishop and Priefts
arriued with the Reliques
at the Monaftery, they
were by the Abbot, and
his Religious, as Iewells a-
boue all valew, moft re-
uerent-

uerently receaued, & vpon
the high Aultar, dedica-
ted to *S. Peter* and *S. Paul*,
magnificently placed, where
many apparent miracles for
the help of foules and bodies, are, to Gods great honour glorified in his Saintes, daily performed: whofe
Name be prayfed for euer
and euer. Amen.

CHAP.

CHAP. XVI.

The Conclusion, of the Transla-
tour, unto this second Booke
of S. Wenefrids *Life, and*
Miracles.

I May fay heere of *S. VVe-*
nefrids miracles (of thofe
later efpecially wrought in
Shrewsbury vpon fuch as honoured the Saint, and were
cured by the vertue of her
reliques) what *S. Auguftine*
in his 22. Booke of the *Citty*
of God, and 8. Chapter, hath
left written of a blind man

mira-

miraculously restored to
sight, and other like miracles done at *Millan*, whilst
he liued there, at the holy
bodies of *S. Geruaſius* and
Protaſius, diuinely reuealed
and tranſlated by *S. Ambroſe*
to another place, as *S. VVe-*
nefrids Reliques were from
Guitherine vnto *Shrewsbury*;
that the Citty, to wit wherein they were done, *grandis*
erat, & immenſo populo teſte res
geſta eſt, was great, and an
immenſe cócourſe of people
able to teſtifie the verity of
them. So as he muſt want

all

all humane fayth, and be obstinatly willfull, who shal refuse to belieue them.

Moreouer I adde, that the Author writing this historie, and publishing the same shortly after these miracles were done, & in the same Citty also; would not for very shame haue written vntruly of them, since not only the Inhabitants therof, but himselfe likewise, certainely had seene and knowne them.

But, as S. *Augustine* complayned of the Gentills in

his

his time, for not belieuing
apparent miracles done at
Saints Aultars, euen before
multitudes of witnesses, and
vpon persons, certainely
knowne to haue bene both
diseased and cured: so may I
heare taxe many Protestāts
of like incredulity, who are
wont to laugh at such vn-
doubted relations, though
neuer so anciently and certainely testified, by no lesse
witnesses then *S. Ambrose*, *S.
Hierome*, *S. Augustine*, and o-
ther holy Fathers, to whom
they vsually giue little credit

dit in such Historicall verities, as they will belieue any
Gentill, or Heathen Au-
thor before them; the which
my selfe haue proued by
many experiences, and for
an example, I will heere
mention one.

It was my chance some
yeares since, to be the guest
of a Protestant Gentleman
in England, of especial note
and ranke in the Countrey
wher he liued, who seing me
one day fixedly to look vpō
a faire picture hāging in his
Hall, wherein the diuers

tor-

torments of some Primi-
tiue Martyrs were liuely represented; Syr, said he, who
can belieue (as for my part
I cannot) that men, to men,
and for Religion only, euer
vsed such barbarous cruel-
ties,& more then butcherly
inhumanities ? To whome
for clearing of so certaine
and testified a truth, I al-
leaged what *Tertullian* in
sundry places of his workes
S. Cyprian, S.Iustine the Martyr, *S. Hierome* , *S. Ambrose*,
and other innumerable Fa-
thers, had either expresly
affir-

affirmed, or suppofed of
thefe Martyrs torments, &
that in bookes either written to the Martyrs themfelues, or to Heathen magiftra-
tes their Condemners; yet
preuayled I nothing, till
calling for *Tacitus*, a Gentill
Author, and moft hatefull
enemy to Chrift himfelfe,
with all fuch as faithfully
profeffed him; I fhewed this
Gentleman what he had left
written of *Nero's* cruelty,
vfed againft Chriftians, by
caufing them to be put v-
pon ftakes in eminét places

of

of *Rome*, cloathed in pitcht shirts, with their armes extended, and so to be fired in darke nights, as torches to the Citty; with other like inhumane torments, exercised vpon them.

Whereupon he began to credit what his Picture represented: and being asked againe by me, why he belieued not before so many testimonies which I had cited vnto him, out of the holy Fathers; he plainely tould me (and it is the common persuasion of Prote-

stants) that most of the Fathers were superstitiously
inclined, and apt to write
Fabulous Legends of Sain-
tes sufferinges, counterfaite
Miracles, and the like, as
themselues ouercreduloufly
belieued them.

With which preiudice of
opinion many, I doubt not,
will come to read this life of
S. VVenefride, & belieue the
lesse of it, as of things done
at home, and long agoe in
our owne Country ; *sed sa-
pientia iustificata est à filijs suis,*
but Gods wisedom & power

mani-

manifested for the glory of
himselfe, in his Saintes , by
such miraculous works te-
stified vnto vs , will by deuout Catholiques be piou<ins></ins>
ly· belieued ; not as pointes
of fayth , diuinely reuealed,
but as pious histories probably written, and worthy
for such to be credited.

The

The End of the second Booke.

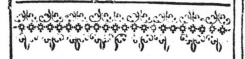

THE
TABLE
OF CHAPTERS
conteyned in this Booke.

THE TABLE

S. We-

S 5   *wrought*

THE SECOND BOOKE

Of

Of

FINIS.

Pſal. 150.

Laudate Dominum in
Sanctis eius.

Prayſe our Lord in
his Saintes.

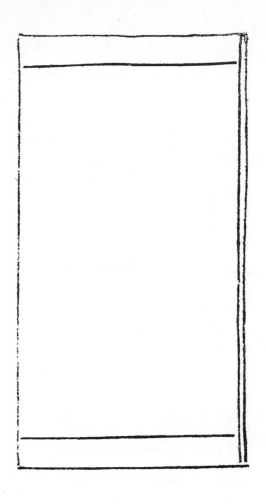

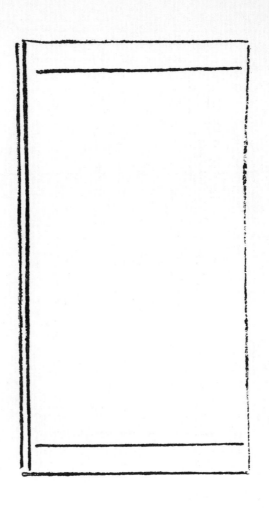